LOVE IS GOD

True Love – True Happiness

For the serious seekers.

Dr. Jean-Francois Orsini, OP, Ph.D.

ISBN:1548397067
ISBN-13:978-1548397067

This book is dedicated to my daughters

- *Caroline Marie Josette*
- *Elisabeth Marie Antoinette*
- *Catherine Jeanne Marie*
- *Marie-Louise Pascale Dominique*
- *Stephanie Marie Emmanuelle*
- *Madeleine Marie Christine*

and their families.

CONTENTS

"God is love"

1 John 4:8

"Be you therefore perfect, as also your heavenly Father is perfect".

Matthew 5:48

"With men it is impossible; but not with God: for all things are possible with God."

Mark 10:27

Foreword

The United States Conference of Catholic Bishops defines the New Evangelization as follows:

> "The New Evangelization calls each of us to deepen our faith, believe in the Gospel message and go forth to proclaim the Gospel. The focus of the New Evangelization calls all Catholics to be evangelized and then go forth to evangelize. In a special way, the New Evangelization is focused on 're-proposing' the Gospel to those who have experienced a crisis of faith. Pope Benedict XVI called for the re-proposing of the Gospel "to those regions awaiting the first evangelization and to those regions where the roots of Christianity are deep but who have experienced a serious crisis of faith due to secularization." The New Evangelization invites each Catholic to renew their relationship with Jesus Christ and his Church."

In other words, this implies that the first effort of evangelization did not achieve the results that were to be expected and therefore a novel approach, or effort, should be implemented anew.

What was not achieved was two things: 1/ combating the crisis of faith in the regions that were initially evangelized and fell victims of secularization and 2/ implementing a first evangelization effort to these areas of the globe still awaiting their first evangelization.

This two-part effort might be facilitated since the world has shrunk following the process of globalization. What may be proposed to the inhabitants of countries where the Christian, and even less the Catholic, culture is not dominant may not be so different from what will be proposed to the inhabitants of the parts of the globe where the Christian culture has been rooted in for centuries. This consequence of globalization should not surprise us as villagers in the most remote regions of China watch American TV programs on their local channels. Translation of these programs is sufficient. "Enculturation" is not really necessary nowadays.

What is essential is to re-introduce these people, no matter where they are making their homes, to Jesus Christ and His Church.

This is the most ardent purpose of this book.

Due to my educational bias, I am motivated to "seek my audience where it is".

When, thousands of years ago, every town, every village, every nation had its own god, or series of gods, a god of the earth, of the sea, of the wind, etc., like the whole cohort of the ancient Greek mythology, spiritually motivated people would be seeking the best god. They would change their god at the drop of the hat if a new god offered better protection against sickness and enemies and provided better chances for bringing them prosperity.

"God is Love" helped the spiritual seekers to understand that there is an inestimable value in choosing a God of love, a God who wouldn't treat them as slaves but as children. A God who is omnipotent and on whom one can totally rely for comfort and inspiration.

First my audience, as I understand it, is not primarily motivated by spiritual values. It is less inclined to look for a new God to worship that many of its ancestors were.

On the other hand, the material world is offering all its trappings aimed at the seekers of love. Advertising, the loudest horn of modern "culture", is not as much addressing the *homo economicus*, the buyer who would seek the best value for his money, as to the *homo socialis* who foremost seeks the company of others who could love him, should he buy the wares offered by the ads. What the latter promises: the best clothes, cars, etc. should certainly bring the love of one's friends and perhaps even the unbounded love of this special one one's heart most desires.

"Love is God" addresses this audience and help it understand that there is another love, a much more intense love, an unconditional love, that is at hand, and free for the asking. The love that is the God of the Christians.

I must state here that a most admired priest wrote to me that "God is Love" is inappropriate. It would be like rendering God into an amorphous, vaporous, love-"Force" as in the movie series *Star Wars*. It would be misleading. He conceded that the title does have a shock value. I missed the opportunity at the time, but I now realize I should have responded that "God is Love" may also be misleading, with my all due respect to St. John Apostle. Out of context, "God is Love" might suggest that Love is the only attribute of God. Actually, God has many more and formidable attributes, including Being (I AM), Truth, Omnipotence, etc.

The great French Dominican, Fr. Henri-Dominique Lacordaire, OP, wrote that there are three types of workers in the vineyards of the Lord: the pastors, the doctors and the preachers. The pastors are shepherds and have to protect their cares from the wolf, the Devil who pushes to sin. Doctors must fight ignorance and their task is to instruct the people. Preachers – which Dominicans are, as the Order of Preachers to which I am most thankful to belong - have to fight against false knowledge. This is more difficult than just to have to instruct people. As it is when children keep asking their parents "why, why", the first explanation is usually easily accepted by them. A second, different, explanation must dislodge the first, as the first explanation has had time to establish strong roots. The truth has an uphill battle to be accepted in the minds of those who were not educated with it.

Thus, a new evangelization is indeed the work of the Preachers. The entire world thinks it knows about the Lord God. My roommate in graduate school was a Chinese who told me that many humans have suffered more than Christ on the cross. For him, that was enough to understand Christianity: we overstated the sufferings of one of the thousands human beings who were crucified, or tortured, over the centuries. Our faith can be dismissed, in his mind.

In order to correct misunderstanding of the faith, this book seeks to address the questions that really matter in order to change attitudes and make converts. I have identified the three questions that I believe hinder the understanding of and therefore the rallying of people to the true faith.

They are:

1/Why would a good God allow evil to exist if He really is a good God?

2/What do you mean that God offers unconditional love when He asks us to follow all these commandments?

3/Why should I entrust to God the good management of my personal life when He makes things so difficult for me, if He exists?

Not only are these questions answered here, the best we can, but each one of them is answered through the very illuminating light of love. Love is the ultimate answer.

I would like to thank all my family and friends for all the love and care they provided me during the writing of this book as well as during my whole life. I would also like to thank the members of the Third Order of Dominicans, Immaculate Conception chapter of the Dominican House of Studies, Washington DC. And the good priests that helped my studies and spiritual life, and especially Fr. Bartholomew de la Torre, OP and Fr. Pierre Conway, OP.

Chapter 1 – The Search for Love

The disorganized search for love

Most of us seek love and we do it in very many different ways. These ways have in common the sad characteristic that they are, to a large degree, inefficient and inefficacious in their quest. Seeking love requires a lot of time and effort, but this time and effort, in the end, do not necessarily yield for us a satisfactory dose of love. Indeed, we seek infinite, or perfect, love but do not find it in our usual different pursuits.

Let's talk first about romantic love since it is probably what comes first in the mind when the word "love" is being uttered.

Loving a person romantically starts with a period of fascination with that person.

That fascination may be in the form of "love at first sight". Barely a few glances and we decide: this person is really my type! "He or she is so much my type that I cannot believe that that person exists. It is a real delight to see that person move around, communicate, and to be near such a charming and endearing person. "It is so good to be around that person that I want to be with that person all the time".

This is one way that one may start to fall in love.

Or this love may be developed over a period of time. For example, a young couple who were in the same university and were already friends, fell in love. The man discovered his love when, in the fraction of a second, he became fascinated to see the young woman handle a hammer quite expertly as they were both involved in a "Habitat for Humanity" project (this group has volunteers together building houses for the poor). While he had not been struck by love before, in one instant this fascination with the hammer expertise of the young lady sort of flicked the switch and he found himself about to fall in love.

Naturally this fascination is not enough. The second movement is called "crystallization". It is when the sauce "takes", we might say. A crystal is formed when minerals are in a liquid form in the proper combination and conditions and in a matter of hours the liquid becomes a solid. The movement of the heart achieves similarly a level of firmness in its selection of the object of its love.

The prevailing sentiment during this phase is: "I cannot believe that other people do not see the wonderful qualities of the object of my love. It is clear that that person is for me. Indeed, I want to be with that person, the two of us only and for the rest of my life".

This movement is important as it will contribute to the necessary and very important element of uniqueness of the spouse and fidelity in the love. Not only does the lover indeed makes a big step in being committed to a single person but, along with that commitment, there is also a commitment to exclude all other persons as truly acceptable for the lover's romantic love.

"This is the only companion I want. I will give everything to be with that person and I want most of all that that person loves me back". This very natural commitment to exclude is the psychological foundation of the more morally and willfully developed later commitment to fidelity toward this person.

Crystallization happens, after the fascination phase, when the would-be lover has been able to do a summary investigation (more or less in depth, depending on his or her personality) that there are no major impediments for this love to be pursued. This is the phase when the loving person allows rationality – as opposed to subjectivity - to have a last chance to be a player in the process: "is there some hidden factor that would make my love impossible and for which I should entirely drop the idea of loving this person".

This investigation is not always well done, especially when the fascination is very powerful. Naturally in a case like that of Romeo and Juliette, from the famous play by Shakespeare, the two had decided that the opposition that their families would make for them to be together was not a major problem. We know that this hasty conclusion by this young, endearing, but naïve couple should not have been made as it led to a very tragic end.

But now the two stages of the romantic love have been complied with. The object of the love then is wooed by the lover. If the object of the love of the lover cannot share the same love, and declare the love unwelcome, the lover is due for a considerable amount of pain. The strong emotional commitment of the lover's heart to loving the chosen one meets a dreadful and crushing wall following the news that his love is not unrequited.

Many a loving heart, at that moment, does not "take no for an answer" and redoubles the efforts of wooing the very desirable object of its love. Some succeed, happily for them. Some others do not succeed who had invested so much emotional effort that, in the future, they might probably not fall in love with the same enthusiasm and generosity as the first time they did fall in love. They might become a bit cynical about love.

Let's consider now the cases when indeed the love was requited and the couple is experiencing the bliss of shared love. This is the honeymoon, which hopefully lasts a lot longer than a honeymoon trip!

But, after a few years – or maybe even months - this starlit romance begins to touch down on the ground of reality. The couple does greatly care for each other, but they find more and more instances when the actions of the other are deemed very unsatisfactory, especially when the outside world starts putting pressure on their day-to-day lives. They have rows, often because of different perspective on how to deal with this outside world, with finances, with children, with difficulties. These rows may become more frequent and more hurtful and, in extreme cases, they pull the couple apart a little more every time they occur.

In view of the statistics, it appears that these rows do all the more often end up in separations and divorces.

What happened to that couple with a past of fascination for each other and crystallization of their loves, and of a successful wooing story?

It is clear that there was some misunderstanding somewhere. A theory on marriage-mending states that in a couple there should be a balance between the input and the output each gets from the marriage. Each member puts in affection, work, understanding, sacrifices etc. When one of the member of the couple decides that the balance is definitely not in his or her favor, that member becomes angry with the perceived injustice. That anger soon comes out on the surface of the couple's relations. The other member begins to develop another anger not appreciating the spouse's grievances because he thought it to be unjustified. And the two angers come to a paroxysm with the conclusion of a separation, and later a divorce. The theory recommends to each member of the couple that they patiently, together, and lovingly, analyze the attitude of each of the two and make the proper adjustments in what they bring to the marriage and what they should expect to take out.

So what really happened? Well what happened is that the couple got disillusioned. They were expecting perfect love and they did not get perfect love. The very nature of each human being is seeking perfect love and when we fall in love we believe that we have found perfect love, until later we must realize that we were wrong to expect such perfect love in the relationship.

One aspect of perfect love is that that love should be unconditional love. To view relationships and love as a contract where there should be some balance between what we bring and what we receive in the relationship is exactly what is not unconditional. If, in a couple, one member measures what he gets back from his love, the love is not unconditional. Measuring the quantities of what one gets back from the relationship means that certain things are owed in the relationship. And, truly, isn't it normal that we get some good things back in the relationship?

If we offer gifts, we would like to hear "thanks" and get a minimum of gratitude. When there are things to take care of, washing dishes, cooking, etc… would like to be the only one to do these chores?

Relationships and married life are absolutely not structured for, nor expected to be, unconditional love. Unconditional love cannot be found in human relationships.

Therefore, in a marriage, each person should understand that they and their partners are only humans who are not capable to give perfect love. If lovers want to be wise in their relationships, they need to realize that when unsatisfied with what they are receiving from their loved ones, they should redouble offering more credit to their spouses, being less demanding towards them, as well as to offer this dissatisfaction as sacrifices for the good of the marriage. If the other gets the clue and does likewise, the relationship will gain a renewed energy. If they believe in God, and therefore in perfect love, it is easier for them because they know the real source from which perfect love is indeed readily available. And their belief in God has told them that only God loves us with perfect love and therefore they possess a wisdom about human loves that saves them from unnecessary break ups.

Let's face it: the human, natural and common attitude is to believe that in a relationship what one offers is more than what it is in all objectivity. We overestimate what we deliver to the other. And, again, it is human to believe that what one receives is really less than it objectively is. We tend to understate what is offered to us. If both members of a couple think with this common and natural attitude, there will definitely be a problem because both will think they have been wronged in an unfair relationship. The two sides did not meet to close the buckle. There will be too much of a distance between what is being exchanged by both and how the give-and-take needs to be in order to satisfy both. Therefore, "working at one's marriage" means that, continually during the life of the couple, both need to be generous and accept that what they receive is enough to satisfy their sense of justice on how the couple should function, and make sure that what they provide is a bit more than what they would think is the normal contribution they need to make for the good of the marriage.

Before we close this section on romantic love, we need to review a dysfunctional phenomenon which we will call Don Juanism, which is the behavior of some to change romantic partners at a fast clip. First, we need to point out that if Don Juan is a male figure for describing that behavior, it has been adopted with gusto by many females in our modern world especially with the advent of the Pill, which artificially removed the natural consequence of sexual relations, namely the procreation of children. See TV programs such as "Sex and the City".

Don Juanism exists on the confused notion that repetition of romances might be necessary to reach and obtain the state of perfect love that is being felt almost at hand at the very beginning of a love relationship. Don Juanism believes it is important to keep trying to get this feeling to be loved by an unconditional love by multiplying relationships. Naturally, after a few such experiments, the hope for this perfect love is severely degraded. It turns into a series of emotionally arid sexual liaisons for which the human motivational quality has progressively been replaced by the mere satisfaction of animal urges, the lowering of respect of the humanity of the other, and, from there, despair of any possibility of attaining any true love.

Unfortunately, romantic love is not the only field where we do not obtain the perfect love we seek for our happiness.

Chapter 2 - Love and Happiness

It has been recognized and taught by philosophers for centuries that there are basically two types of Love. The Love of Friendship and the Love of Desire.

The first is Love for the sake of our friends, for their own good. The Greek had the word "agape" for it. The second is Love of something or somebody for the sake of the good they give us to satisfy some of our desires. When it is love corresponding in sexual desire the Greek called it "eros". Eros alone is not a principle that should lead the good planning for a satisfying life. Eros addresses some of our natural animal material desires and is necessary for the continuation of the species. But there are other material desires. And, more importantly, we need to favor the needs of our non-material side over the needs of our material side. After all, how can we love at all if our heart and our mind does not love?

Love of friendship is a love that is concerned for the good of the friend. When we have friends, who are in a bad spot we want to help them. We are there for them. We want to take care of them when they need care.

When everything is fine with them, we enjoy being with them.

Love is also unitive. We are glad spending some time with our friends. This is why we like to go out with them and go to restaurants and enjoy food together and attend movies together.

But when things are bad we want to make things to be good again for them. If they are sick we want to be with them, even spending long hours in their hospital room, for example. We want to bring them what would make them well again.

This tendency to protect our friends or to make everything good again for our friends can go pretty far. As the Bible says: "Greater love hath no man than for a man to lay down his life for his friends."

Thus, service members in the military are showing a lot of love for their country and fellow citizens. When they sign up, they formally agree to put their lives at risk for them. This is why we need to thank them at each occasion for their services. First, they put themselves at risk during combats for the sake of the citizens of their nation, the great community which they thereby treat as their friends. But second, some are ready to give the ultimate witness of love for their buddies.

Thus, some heroic soldiers have been jumping on grenades to save the lives of their soldier friends. An enemy grenade rolls into an enclosed space such that, when it explodes, most of those in that space will be greatly injured or even killed; someone jumps on the grenade covering it with his body to muffle the explosion so he will be the only one getting the impact of the blast. Even if he is wearing a bullet proof vest, this act leads most surely to his sacrificial death.

Because we often sense we could be totally fulfilled with perfect love, we readily can make the connection between perfect love and happiness.

Indeed, happiness has been defined as the cessation of all wants. Therefore, going along with this definition, if we had perfect love, we would need nothing else.

A quick sidebar here: we do have a great reason to look for happiness in romantic relationships. Many do not know that "sex" comes from the Latin "secutus" which means "cut". The human species – like other species – is cut into two types: the male and the female. Each type feels unfulfilled until united with the other type. In sum, a happy reunion of one of each type, a male with a female, does go a long way to make each one feel more fulfilled and therefore happier.

But beside romantic love, how do we plan and prepare to receive happiness? Are we, in particular, seeking perfect love in an informed, well planned and well executed plan? No. Instead, we fill our daily activities seeking many things in the vague hope of reaching a high state of happiness somehow.

Let's suggest here that there are two paths on which we are spending the most time in seeking happiness. These two paths are the searches for 1/security and 2/entertainment.

Most of us spend a lot of our waking hours making a living, that is earning the money that is necessary to pay for shelter, food, and clothes, for ourselves and for our families. We want to be financially comfortable. Meaning that we want to be sure we can be able to provide all that is necessary for our basic needs and more. In a way we want to return to the mother's womb type of security that materially feels all our needs. But, really, don't we go overboard and try to make as much money as possible? Aren't we workaholics sometimes? Also, haven't we reached a level of frenzy in our habits as consumers?

We seek to follow the latest fashion, replacing good stuff for stuff that is more fashionable. We look at our neighbors and want to make sure that "we keep up with the Joneses". These desires have no limit. We want to live in a palace with all sorts of goodies.

On the other hand, for our free time, we also seek to follow our second path to happiness. We yearn for the best entertainment: we go out, go to bars, eat out, go to ball games, to museums, to movies, to plays, to circuses, to events of all sorts. We take our loved ones there too and share the entertainment value with them. But don't we also overdo it? Don't we get into a frenzy to be happy and have fun?

Now let's test the rationality of the effectiveness of these actions. Let's see what happens to some of our fellow human beings who have achieved the most, who have gained such high income that they can afford the greatest level of security as well as being able to live the life of extreme entertainment. Let's pick an example. Let's look at the life and death of Michael Jackson.

Michael Jackson acquired land in Santa Inez, California, for 17 million dollars. On it he built several theme park rides: a Ferris wheel, a carousel, a movie theater and a zoo among other buildings. For security, he had a staff of 40. That was the Neverland Ranch. The whole operation was evaluated at 100 million dollars in 2003. This, in view of the fact that his income from all sources was estimated at $125 million for the single year of 1989.

Jackson had a great love of money, fame and entertainment. The problem is that all these are contradictory. With money, he could build the biggest "home", this Neverland Ranch, with all his most luxurious fantasies. Most very rich people do build enormous houses with many items of luxury and even features that are elements of their childhood dreams that have come true, like a grotto in the gardens or castle towers as part of the buildings, for example.

However, in such a big home, if one is alone, after a while, life gets to be very boring. So, Jackson had to conceive his home to be able to invite a lot of friends. But Jackson actually had very few real friends. His closest friend was his doctor and the nurse working for the doctor. He later married the nurse. So basically, the people he invited in his "home" in the hope of contributing to his entertainment were strangers. But strangers can be dangerous. Hence the 40 guards to protect him and his toys.

Michael Jackson died from a drug overdose given to him by his "friend", the doctor.

Similarly, very rich people enjoy inviting friends to stay at their big houses but they also install a lot of security features in these homes. The cameras and the watch dogs are to protect them from the world outside. Still they are very much threatened inside their own houses by the dubious characters that are happy to stay on the premises days on end and enjoy the good food, the pool, the entertainment rooms of their hosts' palaces.

Besides weird and fun but very potentially dangerous "friends", one can increase the entertainment value in one's life by using drugs. Drugs can take human beings into a crazy world. Many artists who felt they were not creative enough, including many of today's singers, as well as artists in the past including Andy Warhol and Vincent Van Gogh, were taking drugs to transfer in their artistic work the views that they gained during their drug trips. Naturally drugs are extremely dangerous and the taking of drugs is the opposite of one's objective of maximum security. Drugs kill.

Security and entertainment are contradictory. Drug addicts seek a maximum entertainment from their drugs. But then these drugs are the most dangerous things that threaten their health and their lives.

A few years ago, a very rich man in the small country of Monaco was assassinated by his own body guard – the very person who was responsible for his security. The bodyguard wanted to impress the maid!

The love of perfect security can be traced back to wishing to return to the womb where all was quiet and no danger was perceived. An extreme love of entertainment often indicates a desire to flee one's conditions, to forget oneself and the disillusion one can have with one's person or one's live, and for a while to have one's mind occupied by interesting matters which in no way are sources of danger or difficulty for oneself. This love is called "escapism". Travel to exotic places is often another mode of escapism as it is literally escaping the externals of one's life, however we carry our own personality and our own issues visiting those exotic places and little has changed for us when we return home.

Perfect happiness must be superior to perfect security and to perfect entertainment, as well as to the sum of perfect security and perfect entertainment, which two are actually very hard to bring together.

Perfect love that would bring perfect happiness is not of this world. Perfect love would be unconditional love, a love that no human being can provide. Even love of friendship is somewhat based on expecting our friends to have the same generous attitudes toward us in our times of need, as we do towards them. Still our hearts ache for this unconditional love.

But as we do believe in and have a need for this perfect happiness and perfect love, we naturally seek a higher reality where all the paths to happiness can be combined, where love is unconditional love.

Chapter 3 - The Need for Transcendence.

Some cynics are happy to claim that there is no one above us. There is no God and that we should be satisfied to create our own objectives for our lives and our own rules for attaining these objectives.

Well the cynics may enjoy their view of the world. But they are in a minority.

It is profoundly human to believe there is a transcendent being who is all truth and all goodness.

The work of Sir James George Frazer – *The Golden Bough* – a sociologist of religion, includes the meticulous gathering of data which shows that, for four millennia, human beings believed in the realm of the sacred, the sphere of existence of the deity who had direct involvement in their lives.

Another researcher, Mircea Eliade, searched for a natural explanation for this human trait but could not find any to be offered from any scientific approach.

Robert Spitzer, SJ, Ph.D., in his book *The Soul's Upward Yearning* comments: "As a result, [Eliade] rejects the possibility of finding such an answer from any secular scientific or social scientific discipline (psychology, sociology, anthropology, etc.). Realizing that no combination of natural phenomena could add up to a transnatural or supernatural one, he concludes that the cause must be some *irreducible* presence of the sacred transcendent reality within us."

Eliade calls "traditional man" the manifestation of this attitude of human beings throughout those four thousand years. This traditional man was "homo religiosus". This man believed in transcendent reality, that this reality had broken through in our material world so that there is a process of sanctification of this material world by the work of the transcendent reality. Consequently, there is a possibility for each one of us to draw near to that reality for our own satisfaction and ultimate meaning. This homo religiosus has further a strong concomitant attraction for myths, rituals and holy places.

Father Dominique Lacordaire, OP, was asked why the Christian religion had so many similarities with many primitive religions. Lacordaire answered that this should be no of surprise to us because the need for religion is part of the human condition. When the Jews sacrificed cattle, lambs and pigeons at the time of Christ, many other religions also practiced bloody sacrifices of animals. That does not mean that all religions are equal. The Mayas sacrificed human beings on top of their pyramids until the flow of blood reached the bottom of the pyramid. They started from the excellent premise that nothing has higher value than human beings on the face of the earth and therefore human beings could constitute the best of gifts to the gods, to be followed by a second very poor premise that God wants bloody human sacrifices.

Eliade further proposed that the advent of "modern man" who is much less interested in religion will show the rise of existential anxiety by modern man. This anxiety is derived from the denial of our "implicit intuition of an absolute reality, our transcendent identity and dignity, the potential to encounter transcendent reality, the potential to obtain satisfaction, and the possibility of finding ultimate meaning and fulfilment." He quotes a 2004 study of the

American Journal of Psychiatry which closes on this conclusion:

> "Religiously unaffiliated subjects had significantly more lifetime suicide and more first-degree relatives who committed suicides than subjects who endorsed a religious affiliation. [...]. Furthermore, subjects with no religious affiliation perceived fewer reasons for living, particularly fewer moral objections to suicide. In terms of clinical characteristics, religiously unaffiliated subjects had more lifetime impulsivity, aggression, and past substance use disorder."

Attached to the idea of a transcendent reality is the notion that this reality is the good itself. Plato in his *Republic* told us that we could know this good through questioning and dialectic.

St. Paul further told us that indeed all individuals know the good, and its opposite, through their consciences. For him, even those individuals who were not educated and taught about the proper religion, the Gentiles that is the non-Jews, knew something about good and evil:

> When gentiles who have not the law do by nature what the law requires, they are a law to themselves, even though they do not have the law. They show that what the law requires is written on their hearts, while their conscience also bears witness and conflicting thoughts accuse or perhaps excuse them. (Rom. 2:14-15)

St. Thomas Aquinas, one of the two top theologians of the Catholic Church, made this more explicit. He talked of conscience as being an addition of the love of the good along with a repulsion towards evil, on one hand, and of some general precepts regarding the good on the other hand (all religions and civilizations do not have necessarily the same concept of the good in all points). St. Thomas' philosophical approach is realism: we experience the world through our senses and can abstract further concepts from sensations. Honey tastes good and getting burnt is evil. We can thus learn about good and evil. The understanding of good and evil, and therefore the development of conscience can be related to the natural law. The earthly realities of nature all around us give signs of God's existence through his Providence which naturally sustain all creatures. This providence is rationally understood by men who identify the Natural Law through which Providence is exercised. For St. Thomas, human reason, gratitude for God's Providence, and the precepts of morality combine to constitute human conscience.

Immanuel Kant, the great German philosopher, had a darker view of conscience. For him "The concept of God is the concept of an obligation-imposing subject outside myself" (*Opus Postumum*). From there he developed an ethics of duty and moral imposition from which he wanted intellectually to keep God aside under the false – and artificial - desire to build a disinterested system of ethics. He viewed the beneficent interaction of man with God - although he believed in God himself - as a confusing element in ethics. Consequently, he sought, out of intellectual pride, to build an ethics of pure logic.

The decline of any religious faith does impact not only on individuals but also on cultures. In many European countries an analysis of movies over the last thirty years shows an increase in themes of anxiety and of doom. Entire movies and TV shows are now produced which present the misery of the lives they portray. Even in films with action such as cop and robber movies, the misery seems to be the most important message of the show as this misery affects the good guys and the bad guys equally. A French TV series like "Engrenages" ("Spiral" in the English version), the Belgian series "Salamander" are some examples. In England, "House of Cards" is a very dark string of events for its representation of dysfunctional human characters. It is interesting that in the country of Dickens, who also presented rather bleak lives and surroundings in his novels about a century and a half ago but offered rays of hope and joy, movie producers have gone down so fast losing all hope in the human condition.

Another reflection: even with the loss of the transcendent good, some intellectual and political movements have developed in modern times which are mimicking the ritualism, pomp and sacredness of religion.

First, the religions of the left… under the aspects of Positivism, Communism, Socialism, Humanism.

Maybe the best representative of an effort to establish a complex ritualism of non-religion is Auguste Comte, a Frenchman, founder of sociology. Positivism was his philosophy. The tenets of his "Religion of Humanity", which he thought was necessary to give a moral force to his philosophy, were 1/ altruism (he actually invented that word), 2/ order (born on the same year as the taking of Bastille in Paris, he thought that after the revolution a restatement of order was necessary after all) and 3/ progress (the consequences of industrial and technical breakthroughs for human societies).

The tenets were connected as follows: "Love as a principle and order as the basis and progress as the goal." The Positive stage was his understanding of the three stages of progress for human societies. Human societies were to be developed by science and according to his philosophy of science.

Comte's "Religion of Humanity" had priests who were required to be married because of the ennobling influence of womanhood. There was a catechism and seven sacraments: Introduction, admission, destination, marriage, retirement, separation (at the time of death) and incorporation (3 years after death). He had a calendar of leaders to replace the calendar of saints. Comte naturally placed himself as Pope of this religion. The Goddess of Reason replaced the Virgin Mary.

Auguste Comte influenced many left-wing thinkers. It was in its wake that Darwin's *On the Origin of Species* was written. Karl Marx and Herbert Spencer were also influenced by him. The Brazilian flag proudly carries the words "Ordem e Progresso" (Order and Progress) which are two of the three tenets of Comte's religion of humanity.

Talking of Marxism, the great feast of Marxism in the Soviet Union was MayDay which is in most of Europe and many countries in the world the equivalent of Labor Day in the US. This was supposed to be the day of the worker but was mostly celebrated with the form of a huge military parade, with throngs of troops and new military hardware with trailers carrying rockets. Watching the parade were the top members of the Soviet government. These top Soviet officials changed with new star arrivals and others who disappeared owing to being disgraced at best, executed at worse. Political scientists the world over watched this group of men atop the Lenin Mausoleum and the changes from one year to the next during the MayDay parade, they hoped to estimate the evolution of the government in the Soviet institution, which was not altogether very keen on transparency, by analyzing the leaders that had disappeared and those who had appeared on the podium from the previous year's parade.

The biggest public display of Communist peaceful celebration in France has long been the "Fete de l'Humanité" (Feast of Mankind), which operates like a huge parish Bazaar cum county fair complete with rides and cotton candy for the comrades and their children.

Another example of the desire from non-religions people to develop and display their taste for the sacred and for rituals is the Global Warming crowd and other radical ecologists.

They have a god: Gaia (the goddess earth for the ancient Greeks). They have a supreme principle: "humans are bad for nature; animals and the wild should be venerated and not used by humans; no trees should be cut down". They have a supreme feast: Earth Day. They have several prophets but the major prophet is Al Gore, the former vice president of the United States. They have a doctrine: "the Science is settled: the earth is increasingly warming and humans are responsible for it". Whoever goes against the doctrine is a heretic. They have ways to atone for the sin of pollution, including buying expensive electric cars or hybrid cars. They have their victories over evil as when the pesticide DDT was banned as it allegedly made animal eggs in the wild too porous and fragile, even as DDT was proven to be very effective against mosquitoes, the vectors of malaria that kills millions of humans in third world countries. They have obtained that ethanol be mixed into automobile gasoline even as it is destroying some engines, has lower energetic value than gasoline, and requires more energetic value to produce than it offers, and the price of the tortillas doubled for poor Mexicans.

So, if humans have an irreducible yearning for religion which religion should they chose which can provide them with prefect love, that love that we have called unconditional?

Chapter 4 - The Search for God and the Problem of Evil.

This perfect love, this unconditional love, wouldn't it be God? There is a natural predisposition in all hearts that indeed this is the answer.

But then, just when their hearts are ready to seek God to find perfect love and perfect happiness, most people are confronted with the Problem of Evil.

This problem is usually expressed as: "If there is such a most powerful and most loving God, how come there is evil in the world?"

The problem of evil is a major issue that stops many people to be religious, to follow a religion, to believe in God. The problem of evil is not an arcane issue of theology, it is a very practical and personal problem that impacts many people in their everyday lives and often very violently.

Many people are confronting this problem in a very direct and material way. Some were believers until a tragedy hit them: they lost a child, they are suffering terrible medical issues, they witness the savagery of mass killings of men, women and children somewhere in the world. They learn about the absolute horror of serial killers that take great pleasure in abducting people and torturing them in cruelest ways before they kill them.

So how do believers in a God respond to that?

Let us see what the different responses are that have been given to this problem from the perspective of different philosophies and religions.

The Response from Hinduism

People usually confront more squarely the problem of evil when they are themselves the targets of evil. "Why me?" is often the heartfelt sentiment of a person who finds him or herself in a very dire predicament. This first cry conveys in itself a feeling of injustice. The problem of evil and the problem of injustice (non-equality of status between different humans), although quite different problems, are often intertwined. It naturally makes them more difficult to analyze and resolve. We will review that issue later.

Hinduism in fact views the Problem of Evil as a Problem of Injustice. It is no longer a problem of evil in the abstract but also in all its dimensions, to become of a problem of injustice: "why some people seems to be subject to all kinds of evil, whereas others do not seem to be afflicted to the same degree."

God is omnipotent, omniscient and just. Yet injustice is observed to persist in the world. How is this possible?

One of the Hinduist brand of religion, the Avaita school of Vedanta finds the response in the Brahma Sutra, 2.1.34:

"No partiality and cruelty (can be charged against God) because of (His) taking other factors into consideration."

These considerations are intertwined with the concept of karma. Karma is the spiritual principle of causes and effects where intentions and actions of an individual (cause) influence the future of that individual (effect).

All individuals, according to this religion, have history of the good and evil they have done or have intended and this history conditions what will happen to them in the future.

Hindus also believe in reincarnation. That is, after we die we are reborn into another living creature which can be a man or a beast. A better karma will help reincarnating into another human being. A poor karma will lead to a reincarnation into a person with a more difficult life, or even an animal.

In Hindu society, there are therefore several classes of beings that are regulated by the type of karma they have. Even among human beings there are different classes. These are called "castes". In the higher caste are the Brahmans and the lowest caste are the untouchables – called Dalits. The higher classes cannot touch the untouchables lest they are going to be corrupted by that touch.

So, India has a caste system where a slice of the population is better-off, the Brahmans and several lesser castes, the lowest being the untouchables who are the worst off. These have practical consequences in public policy and practical living. Even at the level of national public policy, untouchable cities and neighborhoods do not receive the same quality of public service as the areas where the better castes live, although in the law of the new independent country with aspirations to be democratic, this injustice is claimed to be illegal nowadays in modern India.

To come back to the problem of injustice, the Brahmans respond to the lower castes: it is your karma, for which you are entirely responsible, that made you be born in that lower caste where you are subjected to all sorts of evils. If you have a good upright life doing the good and willing the good, at your next reincarnation you will be reborn in a better caste, maybe even into the Brahman class.

There is therefore, based on centuries and even millenaries of tradition, a socio-political-religious system that aims to reassure the lower castes that their situation is just, that they should be patient and work hard at doing and intending the good so that they will eventually – after possibly several rebirths - be in the much better position, that of the Brahmans, and thus much freer of the evil of their present conditions.

This system will work at keeping the peace in a society as it requires the lower classes that might otherwise complain to know and keep their place. But India and Hinduism have been in contact with many other cultures and religions. It is not surprising that those who have the worse end of the system have decided that they do not agree to continue playing along. As a result, many Untouchables have converted in mass to Christianity and specifically Catholicism.

Brahmans may be satisfied by the Hindu response to evil but many are those within the Hindu culture that are not satisfied.

The Response from Buddhism

Suddhodana Gautama, Buddha, was a historical young Indian prince whose father kept him within the walls of the palace where the quality of life was fit for a king. But the young prince eventually escaped, jumping over the palace high walls, and witnessed the great evil and poverty of the lives of the great multitude outside the palace. It was such a shock that he decided to go on a spiritual quest.

He had seen in what conditions the majority of Indian society lived under the system of Hinduism and wanted to bring a new solution to that difficult reality.

Buddha tackled the problem of evil from a special -limited – angle, that of the subjectivity of evil: suffering. It is solidly inscribed in the core of his doctrine:

The doctrine is based on the Four Noble Truths:

1. The truth of dukkha (suffering)
2. The truth of the origin of Dukkha
3. The truth of the cessation of Dukkha
4. The truth to the path leading to the cessation of Dukkha

From this it is clear that all concepts, all interrogations, all propositions will be based on the matter of suffering. Practically then, the matter of how to remove suffering must be the urgent road to action.

Accordingly, the fourth truth is composed of the Noble Eightfold Paths:

- Right view (right understanding)
- Right intention (right thought)
- Right speech
- Right action
- Right livelihood
- Right effort
- Right mindfulness
- Right concentration

These eight paths create eight conditions which, when developed together, make it possible to arrive at the cessation of Dukkha, or of suffering.

Naturally "right" is good. Nobody could go against "right". But when the core idea is some concept not more elevated than "suffering", it is difficult to articulate intellectually what is right. There is a lack of perspective. It is difficult to develop an all-encompassing philosophy or ethic to define these rights, if the principal concept is only "suffering".

Instead of reaching for a higher level of abstraction to solidly anchor and define what is right, Buddhism multiplies lower levels of solutions, practical solutions. Buddha grafted on these teachings further refinements such as the "Four Immeasurables":

Thus, the Buddhist devotee is asked to pray:

1. May all sentient beings have happiness and its causes
2. May all sentient beings be free of suffering and its causes
3. May all sentient beings never be separated from bliss with suffering
4. May all sentient beings be in equanimity, free of bias, attachment and anger.

Also the Middle Way teaching is important:

1. The practice of non-extremes, for example: moderation between extreme self-indulgence and self-mortification
2. The middle ground between some views (for example if things exists or do not exist)
3. An explanation of Nirvana where it is clear that all dualities are illusions.
4. A term for emptiness, which is actually a balance between extreme permanence and nothingness.

Buddha conserved the principles of Karma, of reincarnation from Hinduism. The cessation of Dukkha or suffering is the state of Nirvana.

Buddhists practice yoga with many variations but whose spiritual object is meditation. They possess a very strict series of ethical rules but, as we saw, weak definitions of what is right according to these rules, therefore allowing for a wide range of interpretation of these rules.

As we mentioned Buddhism limits itself to the problem of suffering which limits the problem of evil to a subjective perspective, subjective to each individual, without a solid social dimension. It is viewed with a psychological or mental perspective, with little room for the sociological. It neglects the fact that Evil in the world has also objective and social dimensions. How do we explain that animals eat ferociously other animals? That animals get sick and die, that geophysical movements demolish trees and kill animals? Evil is not only limited to the human race, and especially not limited to each individual who wants to banish all evil and suffering in one's life by leading a life of minimum movement, want and undertaking.

Animals, predators as well as preys, were on earth before humans, therefore all the evil on earth cannot all come from humans doing evil things. For individuals trying to pray for a better world and to try to better oneself it would therefore not eradicate all the evil in the world. Or how do animals climb up the scales of the Karma to become humans? (did predators stop predating? did preys offer themselves in sacrifice?). These unanswered questions are conceptual flaws in the body of Buddhist doctrine.

Buddhism is essentially very mental as it is insisting on changes in attitudes. It is also very self-centered. Many stone statues show the Buddha with his eyes practically closed; closed to the outside world in order to better meditate, to be better opened to one's interior self. Meditation is so pervasive as a recommended devotion that it is no surprise that Buddhism has been described as the worship of the belly button.

Any social action to remove the evil of the world is very peripheral to its teaching. Charitable action, love to be brought to the social sphere is very lacking in a Buddhist world. The impact of the work of Saint Mother Theresa of Calcutta had all the more force due to the feature of her Catholic religion which insists in taking care of the poor and the suffering.

In a very shallow fashion, Buddhism favors mild manners, meekness, and lack of doctrinal certainty and lack of ambition. It has had much appeal on the youth of the Western world of the 1960's. These youths had just received The Pill and were looking to put in practice the sexual revolution and they would not accept any stern doctrinal reproach that sexual laxity was to be renounced. They were very responsive to the availability of Tantra Yoga, which brings Buddhism to a very sensual and sexual level. They were also interested in drugs and the hazy formulation of Buddhist teachings were very appealing themes to contemplate during their drug "trips". A lack of entrepreneurial ambition was also appealing to this generation which revolted against what they considered their parents' extreme emphasis on personal acquisitions and the values of the economic development of the '50's.

In all this, in the doctrine and in the practices, we see no interest in reaching for Perfect love. Unconditional love is totally absent from the Buddhist horizon.

The Answer from Islam

In this section I will abundantly use the analysis of Daniel Ali, a proud Kurd who fought the Turks with arms. A former theologian of Islam, he converted first to Protestantism and later to Catholicism and became a theologian of Catholicism. He wrote two books: "*Out of Islam*" and "*Inside Islam – a guide for Catholics*". I am very grateful for his work as well as for his friendship.

Islam is the religion that was instituted from the prophesy of the Prophet Mohammed in seventh century Arabia. He wrote down the Koran as the message that was communicated to him as the verbatim word of God. Consequently, only the Koran wording in Arabic is acceptable to Muslims. Muslims consider that their God, Allah, is the same God as that of Christians and Jews. Many of the sayings of the Koran can be related to Judeo-Christian sayings of the Bible. But they see in Jesus not as the Son of God but as another prophet. Thus Islam denies the whole teaching of the Incarnation. This lead to rejection of the Blessed Sacrament, the Trinity and the Mass. Islam takes pride that it is offering a very simplified religion.

Mohammed is the last prophet before the Last Day of earth at which time Jesus will come down to render judgement. Muslims consider that the sayings of Christ were corrupted and that everyone at the time of Christ was a Muslim but a plot was conceived and executed by Jesus's disciples to corrupt the true religion.

Islam considers that it is of the true essential nature of human beings to be Muslims. Therefore, there is a need to make non-Muslims understand their obligation to relate to their true nature and become Muslims. Muslims should take an active role in the conversion of the whole non-Muslim population of the world by exercising Jihad.

Islam spread very fast. According to Hilaire Belloc's *The Great Heresies*:

> "Mohammed's Arabian converts charged into Syria and won there two great battles, the first among the Yarmuk to the east of Palestine in the highlands above the Jordan, the second in Mesopotamia. They went on to overrun Egypt; they pushed further and further into the heart of our Christian civilization with all its grandeur of Rome. They established themselves all over

> Northern Africa; they raided into Asia Minor, though they did not establish themselves there as yet. They could even occasionally threaten Constantinople itself. At last, a long lifetime after their first victories in Syria, they crossed the Straits of Gibraltar into Western Europe and began to flood Spain. They even got as far as the very heart of Northern France, between Poitiers and Tours, less than a hundred years after their first victories in Syria in A.D. 732."

Islam never developed a complete theology. Mohammed took what he liked from Catholic doctrine and threw away what he didn't like (that's is a radical and subjective way to obtain a simple religion). The primary beliefs are summed up in the *Shahada*, or Confession of Faith: "There is no god by Allah and Muhammad is his prophet." That Confession is recited several times a day by the muezzin during the call for prayer from the top of the minaret, as it replaced the Catholic steeple and the call from church bells, when churches were still oriented towards Jerusalem, "ad orientem", so mosques were oriented toward Mecca.

The Koran alludes to many elements of the Christian Bible but makes serious changes. Islam recounts the story of Adam and Eve in the garden of Eden but with a final twist. "Oh Adam, dwell you and your wife in Paradise and eat with pleasure from its fruits, whenever you want, but do not come near this Tree, lest you become of those who offend" (Sura 2:35). The Koran then recounts that Adam and Eve disobeyed God and ate the fruit of the Tree. "But Satan misled them, expelled them from the place in which they were; and We said 'Fall down each one of you a foe unto the other! They shall be for you on earth a habitation and provision for a time" (Sura 2:36).

In the Christian Genesis Adam blames Eve and Eve blames the serpent. They do not take responsibility for their sin nor do they repent. Their sin brought evil in the world and all the children of Adam and Eve were infected by death. According to the Koran, on the other hand, Adam asks pardon from Allah and Allah forgives. For Muslims this is the end of the matter. There is no Original Sin imprinted on all humans but only the "First" and "Forgiven" sin. Therefore, Muslims do not have to seek their redemption. They are saved from going to hell, provided they satisfy to the Five Pillars of Islam. They do not need baptism to eradicate the Original Sin. They are a Race of Lords far superiors to Infidels.

The five pillars of Islam are:

- Confession of Faith (Shahada).
- Prayer (Salat)
- Fasting (Sawn)
- Pilgrimage (Hajj)
- Almsgiving (Zakat)

Confession of Faith:

As mentioned there is no baptism in Islam. One becomes a Muslim by doing the Confession of Faith in front of Muslim witnesses. The Shahada includes several elements:

- The oneness of Allah
- The confession that Allah should be the only one that humans should adore (this is in opposition to the Catholic doctrine of the Trinity as Muslims claim that Catholics are not mono-theists.)
- The confession of his holy names (which are 99) and his essence.

- The confession that Mohammed is Allah's prophet which implies that all humans must follow Mohammed, the perfect example for all humanity to imitate.

Prayer:

Muslims should pray 5 times a day. It was stated that this is the most important pillar. Muslims can be excused from not observing the other pillars with good reasons, but not this one.

Naturally this is a copy of the Catholic Liturgy of the Hours, prayed as:

Matins (during the night, at midnight)

Lauds or Dawn Prayer or Early Morning Prayer (First Hour = approximately 6 a.m.)

Terce or Mid-Morning Prayer (Third Hour = approximately 9 a.m.)

Sext or Midday Prayer (Sixth Hour = approximately 12 noon)

None or Mid-Afternoon Prayer (Ninth Hour = approximately 3 p.m.)

Vespers or Evening Prayer ("at the lighting of the lamps", generally at 6 p.m.)

Compline or Night Prayer (before retiring, generally at 9 p.m.)

In the Catholic Church, this Liturgy of the Hours needs to be said, using their Breviary, by clerics and religious and lay people are encouraged to pray them.

Fasting.

Ramadan which obliges all Muslims not to consume food nor liquids during day hours, is the Muslim version of Lent but Islam has changed its purpose.

Pilgrimage

At least once in their lifetime, Muslims are expected to travel to Mecca if they can afford it.

Almsgiving

Almsgiving is very similar to the practice of doing Charity to the poor for their sustenance and also for the purpose to clean the heart of the giver.

There are in addition Six articles of Faith that Muslims should adhere to:

- Belief in Allah and his unity (he definitely does not have a son)
- Belief in Allah's prophets. Muslims are told that all of these prophets, including Jesus, were Muslims. The Jewish and Christian prophets' revelations were all corrupted.
- Belief in Allah's revelations (the Jewish Torah and the Christian Bible are corrupted).
- Belief in Allah's Angels. Muslims believe that Mohammed received the words of Allah from the Archangel Gabriel (a take on the Annunciation when the Angel Gabriel announced to Mary that she would be the Mother of God, a landmark of the beginning of Christianity).

The Names of Allah include The Compassionate, The Merciful, The King, The Holy, the Giver of Faith, the

Strong, the Almighty, the Majestic, the Creator, the all-knowing.

"The Loving" does not appear among these names.

Further the nature of Allah is unknowable. Muslims are not supposed to know or love Allah but to obey him. Allah is not a father to Muslims but a slave-master. Allah does not love his subjects nor are they supposed to love him.

Allah is also so much beyond comprehension that he is beyond human reason. It is futile to try to understand him with human reason.

Muslims are to practice Sharia and fight the Infidels. Allah makes abundantly clear that he does not expect the whole world to convert. He clearly admits having created many humans destined to go to Hell. "Those whom Allah wills to guide, He opens their breast to Islam; those whom He wills to leave straying, He makes their breast close and constricted, as if they had to climb up to the skies; thus does Allah [heap] the penalty on those who refuse to believe" (Sura 6:125). Is it all the more surprising that Muslims do not believe in freedom of will for individuals? Nor in democracy?

There are contradictory passages on whether good Muslims should be part of a bloody Jihad. But it is clear when considering the actual historical deeds of Mohammad that he intended to conquer and submit the greatest number of people to Islam and that who would not accept would have to be either killed (with the preferred decapitation method), pay tribute as dhimmis, or exiled.

The simplicity of the religion and the power of the scimitar – the word and the sword - where the most powerful elements of the success of Islam.

Clearly, it is not in Islam that one will find a God of perfect love not would most people on earth would easily accept Islam resolution of the metaphysical problem of Evil.

Evil and Justice

We still need to revisit the problem of Evil.

The problem of Evil is an extremely important problem in the course of human affairs. It is not only a theological problem. It is also – and affecting more people - a social and political problem. It is closely connected with the problem of injustice in the world. It is often presented under a different question: "Why do some people have an easy life – for whatever reason – and others have a much harder life?"

Evil in this world can be dealt with as Hinduism does it and one can explain that the people with a harder life should be patient and work at being good people so they will receive their reward at their next life, after their death and reincarnation. We know how the untouchables, in India, appreciate this argument.

The attitude, before this question, of many of those who do not believe in an afterlife, least of all in re-incarnation, is the following: "There is no second dealing of the cards that each of us receives at birth in this world, therefore we should mandate total equality by political means." Those people come to advocate the socialist and communist solutions: take from the "rich" to give to the "poor": redistribution of wealth. There is indeed some rationality in this attitude from the point of view of where these people come from with their unbelief in the afterlife. (Conversely, we can deduct that many who insist on working for the financial equality of citizens have no faith in an afterlife and in any god).

But socialism and communism contain terrible logical flaws: evil is not limited to being poor. Evil can be from many sources: poor health, looking ugly, having limited intelligence, being too short or too tall, being blind or deaf, having limited education, being born on the wrong side of the tracks, etc. etc. The communist solution does not take care of these other types of evils which often are greater that the lack of money because the people suffering from these limitations, even if they are financially comfortable, tend to believe that if they didn't have these other shortcomings, life would be so much better for them.

And then there are people who are quite well-off (or at least better off) and who do not believe (or do not believe very much) in an afterlife and whose position is: "well that's the way the cards of life were handed out to all. I have my cards and you have yours. Don't bother me!" Indeed, this extremely selfish attitude itself is very evil.

And it seems that this last, minority, group of well-off and non-believing people are the perfect target of the communists and socialists and perfect arguments for their ideologies. Communists and socialists actually tend to put all the people who do not agree with them in this class of selfish people, as strawmen for their attacks!

On one hand, Communists and socialists see themselves opposing a segment of the population that believes in a God and an afterlife. The Communist attitude: these people do not really make any sense to us Communists – they think as the good atheists they are - and can thereby be discredited. Then, Communists and socialists look at a second segment of the population who do not believe much in God and afterlife, like themselves (therefore people they think we can deal with) and who unjustly refuse to share their wealth. Their premises and attitudes make sure that these two groups will be at each other throat until the end of the world.

On the other hand, this analysis shows that in many occasions of political strife there could be a resolution when more individuals on this earth start believing in an afterlife and in the proper God. The God of unconditional love.

Chapter 5 - God Omnipotent

We are looking for a God who will resolve for us the question of Evil. At the same time, we are also looking for a God who will offer us pure love.

We remember how the problem of evil was posited: "How could a Good God could allow evil?". On the level of logic, it is a problem of contradiction. Shouldn't we try to investigate first how a God could be a good God? If God is not a good god, there is no contradiction and a bad god will be comfortable in an evil world.

An additional issue to the question of how God could be a good God is the question of whether he should be omnipotent. If he is a good God but without the power to fight evil because he has limited power, then again there is no contradiction. He would have been unable to have created the whole of creation without evil.

And here we will see that only a God of Love can be so omnipotent.

Second Review of Some Religions

Hindus have several gods. There are also several versions of their religion. In particular, one of the branches of Hinduism, Vishnuism, claims that Vishnu is the supreme god. Another branch, Krishnaism, does not agree and believes that Krishna is the supreme god. Kali is another god, which can be a god of construction but also of destruction.

The result is that, in the end, Hinduism has no clear supreme god. Therefore, there is no omnipotent god. Hinduism actually comprises a great number of religious branches in which practitioners only concentrate on a selected number of gods from among all the gods available to them.

What probably happened in the development of that religion is that over the great number of centuries, a great number of individual human beings, whether victorious warriors, great statesmen, great religious, had such an exemplary life that they provoked a cult that ended up giving them the stature of gods.

Shintoism, the national religion of Japan, which treats the Emperor as a God must also have derived from a very powerful cult of the personality of a great man of national importance which over the years deified him and his lineage as gods, sons of the Rising Sun. Interestingly the sun was also worshipped by the ancient Egyptians, under the name of Ra.

Greek and Roman mythologies also offer a whole array of gods. There were so many gods that some gods were given special powers. Thus, Poseidon (in Greek)/ Neptune (in Latin) had power over the sea and all creatures in it and on it. Poseidon/Neptune is a smaller god under Zeus (Greek)/Jupiter (Latin) the supreme god. Therefore, Zeus/Jupiter may be a supreme god but he does not have all the powers since he shares them with Neptune and many other lesser gods. He is not omnipotent.

A god that is not omnipotent cannot be accused of the presence of evil. He just does not have enough power to fight evil.

So, how could a God of perfect love have the power to deal with evil? To answer that, let's look at the power of love.

Love is Constructive – Hate is Destructive

Love is, in part, defined as a general positive sentiment. This sentiment can be applied to three things: 1/ to people, 2/ to the world in general or 3/ to situations.

When applied to people, love sees the best in them and is able to strongly appreciate that what it sees is the best in them.

Bob is a young man with Down syndrome. On him the syndrome is strongly marked. His eyes are slanted. His cheekbones are protruding. His face is round. Any stranger that sees Bob immediately perceives the condition of Bob. John does not have a generally positive sentiment towards Bob. His brain flags Bob as different, as someone who is so obviously damaged that John does not want to have anything to do with Bob. Mary, on the other hand, has a generously loving general attitude and does recognize Bob as someone affected by Down syndrome but she also immediately perceives and appreciate the fact that Bob, like most Down syndrome individuals, has a very joyful and endearing attitude. Because of these last traits in Bob, Mary's view of Bob as a Down syndrome victim recedes in the background. She enjoys having met Bob and having company with Bob. Mary is a loving person.

When applied to the world in general, to have love is to have a very positive sentiment towards the quality of the world, the greatness of the human race, the beauty of the material world, including the earth, landscapes as well as the marvels of the animal world. Love of the world also includes a positive sentiment towards the origin of the world, the good purpose of its creation and therefore be ready to accept the existence of a loving God who is the world's creator.

John has a hard time waking up in the morning. His days seem to him to be a long stream of boring hours, with here and there some elusive moments of unexpected pleasantness. These are shadowed, in return, with extreme moments of panic when things turn out for the worst for him. John's mental condition is basically a latent depression. Mary could not be happier in the morning with all the things she looks forward to do and enjoy. She indeed has a constant list of things to do, to explore, to discover. Life is so exciting to her; she is never bored. She has little time to think of herself. When they come, she pushes aside any inconvenience in her life as flees she can easily brush away.

When applied to situations, a person who has love sees the positive in situations. Love is optimistic. When non-loving persons see that the glass is half empty, loving people see the glass half full.

John freezes when a difficult situation happens to him. Even before formulating a plan to resolve the problem he has little hope that a solution can be found. He does not see the good in resolving problems. "What if I resolve this problem! It would be no good because another one will plague me" is what he really thinks. So, no need to rush and try to solve the problem at hand. Better sweep it under the rug and thus contribute and reinforce in one's mind that things are worse than they appear. Mary, on the other hand, is somewhat of a task oriented person: she not only enjoys resolving problems but rather she actually seeks them out. She keeps constantly improving things around her in the circles of life, be they material things, like the arrangements of her home, or intrapersonal relations, like issues at work or with her friends. She is also thinking at gnawing problems that affect the world at large. She is always proactive, creative, innovative and even entrepreneurial.

Winston Churchill, the great British statesman is quoted as saying: "a pessimist sees the difficulty in every opportunity; an optimist sees the opportunity in every difficulty." A loving person is a natural problem solver and is most likely to undertake constructive projects because he can easily visualize its happy achievement and is not frightened by the difficulties of the undertaking.

Hate is easily viewed as a very negative sentiment. It can also be applied to people, the world in general and to situations.

Hatred of people is manifested with a sentiment that sees no values in individual beings. The so-called hate crimes are perpetrated when the hater meets some individuals belonging to a class that the individual abhors. It may be race, culture or any other trait that sets a fraction of humanity apart from the whole of humanity. The hating individual will not see in those people's traits the trait he would otherwise appreciate in non-members of this group. Hate prevents him from perceiving that these people are intelligent, hard-working, wise or any similar quality. His class hate blinds him to acknowledge positive traits in that person.

Hatred of the world is manifested in the perception of only the negative in the world – usually on centers of the life of the hater. Life is not good to him, there are many more problems than satisfactions. "Endless suffering is the fate of all creatures, and then they die" is one way such people describe the world in which they live and they feel they have to confront every day of their lives. Stupidity is the hallmark of the people around them. Nature is harsh and foreboding. The human condition is meaningless.

So, with this perspective on difficult situations the hating person is not really hopeful that he will be able to resolve them. Their intrinsic difficulties are overwhelming. He is certainly not an optimist regarding these difficulties. Nor is he prepared to undertake any constructive project which will appear to him only as a long sequence of heartaches and frustrations.

All constructive actions in the world are products of love, of loving individuals, of individuals who were able to show enough love to be constructive. But from where does their love comes from?

A God of pure love would be infinitely loving for pure love has no limits. That would make Him infinitely constructive. He would thus be a God creator. He would have created all things, nature, animals and humans. It does follow that He must be an all-powerful therefore unique God, an omnipotent God.

He should have a solution for the problem of Evil.

Would the Christian God be such a god?

Chapter 6 – The Christian God Dealing with Evil

Evil has entered the world through sin. We need to take a historical approach to show that, at every step, a most loving God has shown his love while dealing with sin and evil.

Creation

Back to the very beginning. God created the world. He did not need to create the world, even prompted by his own love. God is perfect and needs nothing. He did not need to create the world. He did not create the best world possible either, for he could have created a still better one. He has total freedom. But he created a good world. "God saw all that He had made and indeed it was very good" states the book of Genesis (Gen1:31). St. Paul insisted: "Everything that God created is good" (1 Tim.4:4). God could not create a world that contained any evil.

The Council of Trent in the sixteenth century, which was a conference of Catholic bishops to correct the errors of the Reformation, had to combat the position of John Calvin and condemn his idea that "it is not man's power to make his ways evil, but that God performs the evil works just as he performs the good, not only permissively but also properly and directly, so that Judas' betrayal no less than Paul's vocation was God's own work." The Christian God, at least in the Catholic view, cannot perform any morally evil act. Calvin thought that, in order to make God all powerful, he should make Him capable of evil too. But God cannot go against His own nature which is goodness and love.

Then, the Catholic doctrine teaches that God keeps all his creation in a continual effort.

Scientists these days have created the concept of "entropy". Entropy states that all systems, with the passage of time, tend to fall apart. Catholic Church doctrine agrees. Living creatures are born, grow and die. Even the mineral world and the stars do not have a limitless duration. God is there at all times to keep all his creation in existence. That is part of Divine Providence.

God is not what a Baroque philosopher, Spinoza, thought He was: a "great clock maker". That is, a force who made the world like a clock maker makes a clock, and when he has finished his complicated work, he walks away from it, letting his creatures manage for themselves on their own power.

First, God does not abandon human beings for He is an all loving God. Second, his creation, including human beings, does not have the power of self-existence. We owe our existence at every moment entirely to God. God could withdraw in a split second his decision to support anything and everything in the world and each thing or the world in its entirety would immediately vanish. Third, God is immanent, that is to say He is everywhere in His creation. He is very close to us and that's how He wants to be. He is close to us because He loves us. Love is unitive.

> "indeed he is not far from us, since it is in him that we live, and move and exist, as indeed some

of your writers have said: We are all his children." (Ac. 17-27-28)

In Genesis, God first created his angels. They are spiritual beings, therefore do not have a body. They are also eminently simple as they do not have any parts. They are very superior creatures. God gave them free will, including the power to choose. The most beautiful angel was called the bearer of light: Lucifer.

Then God created the first humans, Adam and Eve. They had bodies and inhabited a material world which was perfect, Paradise. But they were not superior beings as the angels were. However, like the angels, God gave them freedom of will.

God asked the angels to put themselves at the service of human beings, their inferiors. Lucifer and some other angels refused to serve human beings out of pride. "Non serviam" he said. I will not serve. They refused to obey; they had made a free-will choice; they opposed the will of God; they became demons. Lucifer became Satan. As angels have no parts, the angels who followed Satan became simply, entirely, bad.

Evil for the first time came into the creation which had been all good until then.

Satan induced Eve to eat the forbidden fruit of the tree of life. God had invited Adam and Eve to partake of all the goodness of Paradise, except for the fruits of The Tree of Life. Eve got Adam to also eat the fruit. Adam and Eve disobeyed God. They opposed God who is essential Goodness. They had slighted the God of Goodness. They had committed the Original Sin. Evil came to them and changed their fundamental nature, the nature of all human beings. They were chased from Paradise. Outside Paradise, evil will be their constant companion.

Their living condition on earth and of all their descendants will be marred everywhere and at all time with evil.

Love and Free Will.

Evil did not come from God. It came from an absence, an imperfection, a bad choice. Lucifer and the fallen angels and Adam and Eve did not accept the goodness of God's desire and command. They created a blemish, a crack, in the goodness of the creation. They used their God given power to choose and they used it to make the wrong choice.

They made that choice because God gave them the power to make that choice.

God gave them that choice because of love. God's creation was a creation of pure love. He wanted his intelligent creatures, angels and human beings to share in this world of love as He loved them very dearly. In return God expected angels and humans to love Him and all His goodness, because it is the nature of love.

But love cannot be coerced. God who had made no place for evil in His creation, expected a full and sincere love from angels and human beings. So, he gave them free will so angels and humans could love Him freely and therefore genuinely.

God who is pure love knows perfectly the nature of love: love must be a free movement of the mind and of the heart toward the object of love.

> "Thou shalt love the Lord thy God with thy whole heart, and with thy whole soul, and with thy whole mind." (Matthew 22:37)

Redemption and the Cross.

The actions of Adam and Eve had committed a terrible disorder in God's creation that, until then, was all good. They had introduced evil. Adam and Eve and the human race had insulted the goodness of God who had been terribly affronted.

But the human race is just too insignificant compared to God to present a valid excuse, and to perform an act of obedience to expunge the disobedience committed by Adam and Eve. Only someone at the level of the dignity of God could present a valid apology and an act of obedience to pay back the debt of honor.

God sent his son Jesus to ask forgiveness and pay God back.

As he had the double nature of true God and true Man, Jesus had the required dignity to present an apology to God the Father, and His human nature allowed Him to make it in the name of humans.

The act of obedience consisted in the whole life of Jesus on earth, but was exemplified by the words He said in the Garden of Olives before His arrest:

> "Father, if thou wilt, remove this chalice from me: but yet not my will, but thine be done." (Luke 22:42)

The act of compensation was Jesus' horrible but magnificent death on the Cross.

> "we were reconciled to God by the death of his Son" (Romans 5:10)

This act performed by God, Jesus, the second person of the Trinity is a pure act of love. Jesus did it to obey His Father who wanted to give this expression of His love for us.

> "For God so loved the world, as to give his only begotten Son; that whosoever believeth in him, may not perish, but may have life everlasting". (John 3:16)

The Establishment of the Church

While Adam and Eve had the Devil to advise them, Jesus made sure that humans would have a very powerful and near advising body. He established His Church, the Catholic Church for that purpose.

> "Thou art Peter; and upon this rock I will build my church, and the gates of hell shall not prevail against it." (Matthew 16:18)

His Church kept the Treasury of the Faith intact with the infallibility of the head of the Church, the Pope, speaking authoritatively when doing so "ex cathedra". So the doctrine would not be perverted. Further, the Church offered the faithful the Sacraments to strengthen them, especially the Blessed Sacrament. This Eucharist reconnects us directly, as time in this matter is suspended, to the very sacrifice that Our Lord Jesus made on the Cross, and still has the same value as the historical sacrifice.

> "For as often as you shall eat this bread, and drink the chalice, you shall show the death of the Lord, until he come". (1 Corinthians 11:26)

These two gifts that Our Lord left to us are further and incredibly precious acts of love that He provided us with as He cared about our weaknesses and the support we needed.

Regrettably, we must here note that all these acts of love from God are fully perceived only through the Catholic Church.

Our elders in the faith, the Jews, do not recognize Jesus as the son of God and therefore do not appreciate the love of God that He expressed through the Redemption. For the Jews, God is a very stern God who will principally care for only a small section of humanity, the Jews. But not just now yet. They still have to wait for the arrival of the Messiah! And this in spite that Jesus, in many instances, quoted the ancient Scriptures to show that he was acting in direct line with the teachings of the Torah and they really should have recognized Him as the Messiah.

> "And beginning at Moses and all the prophets, he expounded to them in all the scriptures, the things that were concerning him." (Luke 24:27)

Nor do our Protestant brothers recognize the legitimacy of the Catholic Church, established through the valid succession of Our Lord's own apostles and its unique power of infallibility that protects against heresy and the wonderfully beneficial sacraments that she offers, especially the Eucharist, the living flesh and blood or Our Lord.

They do not appreciate the love of God that comes with this gift of the Church. They do not see how loving is God who gave us His Church, the Catholic Church, to stand against all errors that human beings can get into, and against the weakness of human beings who, like Peter, are often likely to denounce Him. This attitude that Protestants have has an implied consequence: God must be unloving for having abandoned His people for 1500 years or so before a Luther could get the Christian world back on the right path. Also, Protestants must believe that God cannot be taken at His word when he stated that he would establish His Church. God had to wait on Luther and his imitators to establish the real churches.

> "And I say to thee: That thou art Peter; and upon this rock I will build my church, and the gates of hell shall not prevail against it." (Matthew 16:18)

As a consequence, the teachings of Protestants churches vary from one to the other in perfect cacophony, with their only clear unity being their rejection of the Catholic Church.

Judaism and Protestantism do relate to the God of Love but in imperfect ways. To fully understand God's love and to find the pathways to a life lived in fuller union with God and consequently to benefit of the earthly as well as eternal graces that comes from this more perfect union, one needs to learn the complete teachings of the Treasury of the Faith from the Catholic Church.

Chapter 7 - Unconditional Love and Natural Law

It has now been established that nowhere else can pure love be found other than from following the Catholic Church and its understanding and worship of God.

As has been remarked before, one frequent human objection to believing in a God of love is the problem of evil. We have started to deal with that matter and will continue in the next chapter. But we need to recognize another similar psychological hurdle.

And that is: How can we dare say that the God of Catholics offers unconditional love when the Catholic Church is known for so many behavioral and moral requirements she expects from her flock?

The Church commands that sex should be reserved to duly married couples of different genders. Abortion is a strict no-no, etc. etc.

Actually, many would be surprised to know that such attitudes are as old as the Roman Empire. Romans were a very tolerant lot as far as religion was concerned. They had a very large building, in Rome, with a very impressive dome, a marvel of architecture, called the Pantheon. The name of this building actually comes from the Greek language and means: all the gods. When Christianity first arrived in Rome, the authorities were quite indulgent and said to the Christians: "Feel free to bring the statue of your god and we will find a place for it with all the others in our Pantheon."

However, after a while, the same authorities started to realize that not only satisfied with having a quite different god, Christians had also altogether different doctrines from the Romans and most other religions represented by the statues in the Pantheon.

These doctrines were demanding, and included concepts like chastity, humility, generosity to the poor etc. The authorities were not amused. Christians were viewed as insulting to the Roman way of life and that was not acceptable.

Persecutions of Christians started soon after this realization that Christianity had an altogether different set of rules for its followers.

The first part of the response to this concern is that, with these rules, God, through His Church, is not demanding something from us for His own benefit. God possesses total happiness and nothing that we can do or give Him will change in any way His perfect happiness. God is not like a spouse who wants something from the relationship such as a spouse in a human couple would.

The second part of the response is that, actually, these requirements from God – these commandments – are for our own good. And God makes these requirements out of love for us. It is like a mother who would tell her child: "Do not run with scissors!", "do not play with matches", "do not get too close to the cliff". The mother does not make the demands to her child to make the child's life miserable, but she does it out of love. She personally gets nothing out of it, save for the knowledge that in respecting her demands the child will be safe.

We would not think that the mother is being demanding and unloving. But on the contrary, we would consider that she is a good mother who takes care of her children properly. Similarly, when God tells us to do such and such, it is to keep us safe, morally and spiritually but often also physically and sociologically.

To explain this, we need to examine what is called the Natural Law. Just as the child may not realize that while running he can fall on the scissors in a way that they can stab him, or that his foot can slip on a loose rock so that he can fall off the cliff, the adult may not realize that there are spiritual and natural dangers of which he is not aware.

The child may not be aware of the laws of kinetics that would stab him should he fall on the scissors, or the laws of gravity that would kill him should he drop from the cliff. But there are many other laws that humans are subjects to that have been integrated into the nature that God has created as an environment for men. These precisely form the Natural Law.

St. Thomas Aquinas distinguished between four types of laws: the divine law, the eternal law, the natural law and the human law.

The eternal law is identical to the mind of God as seen by God Himself. The divine law is derived from the eternal law insofar as it appears to humans especially through revelation. The natural law derives from the divine law. And human law is the law that humans conceive for themselves and which should be derived from the natural law.

The human creature is subject to divine providence which has disposed the totality of creation towards the survival of humans as well as their reaching their ultimate end, which is life everlasting in heaven. Natural Law therefore spans a whole continuum ranging from physical laws to biological laws, from anthropological laws to moral and ethical laws.

St. Thomas for example explains that human couples should not divorce. In nature, he explains, parents of animals abandon their offspring when the latter can fend for themselves and do not need their parents any longer. However, human children will need their parents all their lives, as well as during the lives of their parents.

Babies should not be aborted because they are already given a soul by God and are full human beings. Abortion is murder. Murdering one's own child, in addition, does terrible physical, psychological and spiritual damage to the mother. It also damages the couple, the family and society as a whole.

Human laws should not go against natural laws because they will be against the true advantage of each one of us.

What could be viewed as stern laws of the Church as willed by God are in fact loving practical proofs of God's unconditional love in all the little and humble aspects of our lives.

Chapter 8 – What do We Learn from the Catholic Church.

We have seen that the chief attribute of God, as taught by the Catholic Church, is that He is most loving. He is offering the purest love which is the objective we seek. We will now have to learn from this Catholic Church how to fully grasp one of the problems that have prevented some to believe in God and what else needs to be done to fully feel this purest of Love.

Evil and Free Will

The Christian God is all love. Therefore, how is the problem of evil resolved with a God of love, on one hand, and the reality of evil in the world on the other hand?

We need to follow the narrative of the Church.

First point. God is not the source of any evil but of all good.

Second point. evil is the consequence of sin, starting from Original Sin.

Third point. Just as, at the time of the creation, God wanted to give human beings free will, God wants each human being now to have the freedom to recognize Him and love Him as Lord and Father. We are therefore to understand and accept the plan of Redemption that had been accomplished by His Son, the second person of the Trinity: Jesus Christ.

But if the whole human race has been offered redemption, individual humans need to be saved one by one.

If God had banished all evil from the world upon the Sacrifice of the Cross and thereby saved us from punishment including damnation, we would not be able to love God back properly.

If we saw God as He is there would not be the need of faith, nor of hope nor of choosing to love. We would be overwhelmed by the glory, the goodness, the love and all the attributes of God. There would not be a possibility to practice our freedom of will. There would not be a possibility to offer God a freely chosen, therefore genuine, love back to Him.

To accept the plan of Redemption means accepting the sacrifice of the Cross. It means being totally grateful for Jesus' sacrifice on the Cross. As love unites, it also means a willingness to associate ourselves with that preeminent act of love of Our Lord Jesus on the Cross.

Jesus redeemed us by taking upon himself the full punishment for our sins, for the sins of each one of us. For that he suffered great pain and insults. He suffered great evils. Evil is still in the world for us to meet this evil in the same spirit that Our Lord met it by fighting the consequences of sin.

Thus, we show our free love to God, by joining Jesus in accepting and dealing with evil in our lives as it is God's will that we do so. We accept our crosses, our personal, close and continual contact with evil, with patience, love and gratitude.

Gratitude because we have been told that, even though our personal cross will be heavy, individually we will not be subjected to having to bear a cross that is too heavy for each one of us:

> "You can trust that God will not let you be put to the test beyond your strength, but with any trial will also provide a way out by enabling you to put up with it" (1 Corinthians 10:13)

If there were no evil in the world any more, we would not be able to show our gratitude and love of God, we would not be able to be fully saved. God allows evil to still be around for a better good, that we all can be saved and join Him in heaven where evil will be no longer.

This explains how there is evil in a world that was created by a God who is all good, as He allows this evil to perdure until the end of time for our own good.

We have now that first understanding of why there is still evil in the world by connecting the existence of evil and the demands of love. We will no longer refuse to believe in God because of the problem of evil.

But we still need to have a better understanding of evil and our objectives to see how we can gain pure love.

Evil and Sin

We have stated that evil is the consequence of sin, but what then is sin?

Is the Devil pure evil? The answer might surprise many. No the Devil is not really pure evil as we might imagine.

God made one of the best angels and gave him the greatest qualities. He was called Lucifer, the bearer of the Light. But, as He has done for all His intelligent creatures, God gave Lucifer free will. Specifically, He asked all the angels to serve all human beings. Lucifer and many lower angels refused.

They opposed God, the source of all goodness. As a consequence, goodness came out of their substance. But they were allowed to still exist, with an existence that is given by God. Demons are not responsible nor the authors of their own existence. God kept the devils around as they are useful in His plan of salvation. Devils are angels without goodness.

Evil is opposition to God and refusal of His Goodness. Evil has no existence of its own, it simply is the lack of goodness.

This observation is interesting about angels, but it is however extended beyond angels. It applies to human beings also.

Blessed Anne-Catherine Emmerich was a German nun who had a greatly spiritual life. She lived at the end of the 18th and beginning 19th century as a sacrificial soul. She had many vision of sacred things, including a very rich and detailed vision of the life of Our Lord and Our Lady as if she was there in person. She had answers to many spiritual questions.

One of them is a question that all people might have asked themselves either in order to better understand Christian doctrine or because they really are eager and have an urgent need for an answer to that specific question.

The question is: how could some souls go to heaven and enjoy forever perfect happiness when they would know that some of their family members and friends whom they knew and loved on earth, are now in hell?

During her visions, Bl. Anne-Catherine obtained the response to that question: before sending them to hell, God would retrieve from these souls all the goodness that He had put in these persons at the time of their conception. These souls have rejected God and His goodness and therefore automatically all goodness would be removed from them as a logical and direct consequence of their rejection of God. They would will become sorts of paper wrappers, good only for the fire. The souls in Hell would completely stop being lovable. Only God, who is all goodness, is lovable in Himself.

Now this should give us a very solid understanding of what we, human beings, are all about. Doesn't it?

At the time of our conception, God somehow "loaned" us some of His goodness, including many intellectual talents and physical traits. Naturally, without these talents and traits we would first begin to be unrecognizable.

Now all the above points point to the fact that we do not really understand what human beings are, until we can place them in their whole history as God's creatures.

Redemptor Hominis

St. Pope John Paul II wrote in 1979 the encyclical – a formal form of a Pope's teaching – *Redemptor Hominis*.

In this most valuable message from the Holy Pontiff, we read great information of what we are and what we should strive for:

> "Man cannot live without love. He remains a being that is incomprehensible for himself. His life is senseless, if love is not revealed to him, if he does not encounter love, if he does not experience it and makes it his own, if he does not participate intimately with it. This, as has already been said, is why Christ the Redeemer 'fully reveals man to himself'. If we may use the expression, this is the human dimension of the mystery of the Redemption. In this man finds again the greatness, dignity, and value that belong to his humanity. In the mystery of Redemption man becomes newly 'expressed' and, in a way, is newly created. He is newly created! 'There is neither Jew nor Greek, there is neither slave nor free, there is neither male or female, for you are all one in Christ Jesus'. The man who wishes to understand himself thoroughly – and not just in accordance with immediate, partial, often superficial, and even illusory standards of measure of his being – he must with his unrest, uncertainty and even his weakness and sinfulness, with his life and death, draw near to Christ. He must, so to

> speak, enter into him with all his own self, he must 'appropriate' and assimilate the whole of the reality of the Incarnation [the second person of the Trinity taking a human nature as Jesus] and Redemption in order to find himself. If this profound process takes place within him, he then bears fruit not only of adoration of God, but also of deep wonder of himself. How precious must man be in the eyes of the Creator, if he 'gained so great a Redeemer', and if God 'gave his only Son' in order that man 'should not perish but have eternal life'.
>
> "In reality, the name of that deep amazement at man's worth and dignity is the Gospel, that is to say: The Good News. It is also called Christianity."

First and essentially, each person should not understand him or herself according to the criteria of the world, but according to his or her nature as a Child of God. If we want to understand more thoroughly where our need for love comes from, as well as how to be able to satisfy this need, we have to learn about the true context in which we were created and in which we live, we have to learn about our true nature, about another set of qualities that we are capable of possessing and need to be possessing and we have to start on the path of acquiring these qualities.

For that we need to know some more about our Creator.

Chapter 9 - The Attributes of God and What They Mean for Man.

The first Vatican Council in its *Dogmatic Constitution on the Catholic Faith* tells us about God:

> "The holy, apostolic Roman Church believes and professes that there is one true and living God, the Creator and Lord of heaven and earth. He is almighty, eternal, beyond measure, incomprehensible, and infinite in intellect, will and in every perfection.
>
> Since he is one unique spiritual substance, entirely simple and unchangeable, he must be declared really and essentially distinct from the world, perfectly happy in himself and by his very nature, and inexpressibly exalted over all things that exist or can be conceived other than himself."

We are looking for a God of true love to exist and be the supreme ruler so that His love will be readily available. This declaration confirms that this is the case as everything falls in place. He is the supreme ruler as the Creator. He is almighty. He is the Creator because He his supremely loving hence positive. He is supreme ruler because He is one, in three persons.

What interest us here is that He is infinite; His will and His love are infinite. He is the source and the giver of the pure love that we seek.

But there is something else we need to conclude: not only is He is pure love, meaning there is no evil and hatred in Him; He is also all the love in the universe. The totality of love. Again, that means that the love in each one of us is also of God.

Does that mean that we are partly God? No.

That means that each of us of us have been given, on loan, an amount of love, just as we also have been given an amount of other qualities.

The philosopher tells us that love seeks the good. God is also infinite goodness. All the goodness that is in us – as well as in the entire creation - is of God.

As we have seen, above, we also have been given, on loan, certain amounts of goodness, that is of qualities such as intelligence, beauty, gentleness, charm, health, etc. etc.

Exercising these qualities is good; using these qualities positively is good; they are of God.

But the very ideas we have of exercising these qualities are also good; they are also of God.

So if those are all of God, what are our merits? How do we exercise free will?

Here is the answer: using our qualities, we are constantly moved to make decisions to utilize positively these qualities. These decisions may seem to be purely outside the moral domain but many are really inside a moral/spiritual domain

If I move a chair back under a table, that seems to be a little thing but it helps the room be more tidied up for others. If I turn off the light leaving a room, I am saving some of God given resource. If I say a kind work to a person that needs it, naturally that is a good thing too and indeed something with a moral quality.

Now the exercise of free-will is such that, as a response to these good impulsions, we may decide not to follow them. If the impulsion to do a good thing is of God, the decision to resist that impulsion is not of God. It is of us. It is sin of omission. If the impulsion is to avoid to do a bad thing is of God, the decision to resist that impulsion is not of God. It is of us. It is sin of commission.

And in many cases, the resistance against doing a good thing, or, conversely in favor of doing a bad thing, not being of God, is evil. It is a sin. Now, there are different qualities of sins: venial sins and mortal sins. Only mortal sins make us loose the friendship of God. Thank be to God, for most of our sins are venial sins.

We should not lose hope too fast as it is said that even saints sin "seven times each day". Most of us commit many more and we are still in God's good graces. We should not be too scrupulous and lose heart but we certainly should realize that we have a long way to go to become saints.

So how do we gain merits in the eyes of God: it is when we do the good things and avoid the bad things, He prompt us to do or to avoid.

But how come a just God will expect many good things from all people when He has put on loan in each of us so many different things and in different quantities?

The parable of the talents.

> "It is like a man about to go abroad who summoned his servants and entrusted his property to them. To one he gave five talents, to another two, to a third one, each in proportion to his ability. Then he set out on his journey. The man who had received the five talents promptly went and traded with them and made five more. The man who had received two made two more in the same way. But the man who had received one went off and dug a hole in the ground and hid his master's money. Now a long time afterwards, the master of those servants came back and went through his accounts with them. The man who had received the five talents came forward bringing five more. "Sir," he said, "you entrusted me with five talents; here are five more that I made." His master said to him, "Well done, good and trustworthy servant; you have shown that you are trustworthy in small things; I will trust you with greater; come and join in your master's happiness." Next the man with the two talents came forward. "Sir," he said, "you entrusted me with two talents; here are two more that I have made." His master said to him, "Well done, good and trustworthy servant; you have shown you are trustworthy in small things; I will trust you with greater, come and join in your master's happiness." Last came forward the man who had the single talent. "Sir," said he, "I had heard you were a hard man, reaping where you had not sown and gathering where you had not scattered; so I was afraid, and went off and hid your talent in the ground. Here it is; it was yours, you have it back."

> But his master answered him, "You wicked and lazy servant! So you knew that I reap where I have not sown and gather where I have not scattered? Well then, you should have deposited my money with the bankers, and on my return, I would have got my money back with interest. So now, take the talent from him and give it to the man who has the ten talents. For to everyone who has will be given more, and he will have more than enough; but anyone who has not, will be deprived even of what he has. As for this good for nothing servant, throw him into the darkness outside, where there will be weeping and grinding of teeth." (Matthew 25 14-30)

This parable – a means for Jesus to teach us a lesson – has several meanings. But it is clear that one who has more talents is expected to produce more. The servant with the two talents who produced two on his own received the same compliment and was told by the master exactly what the master told the servant with five talents who produced five more on his own. However, the servant who did not use his talent had his talent removed; his soul became empty of the talents/qualities that he was given at birth and became the empty wrapper good for the fire of hell.

Therefore, the qualities/talents that Jesus give us at birth are in expectation of the merits that one needs to gain in our lives. The persons who have "everything to be happy" in their lives, and then just sit on their good fortune and do not gain spiritual merits are basically burying their talents. Those on the other hand who have had few good things at birth and manage to lead an honest life have earned many talents.

But what are these merits we are talking about?

Chapter 10 - Our Mission on Earth

What does God want from us?

> "Man is created to praise, reverence, and serve God our Lord, and by this means to save his soul. The other things on the face of the earth are created for man to help him in attaining the end for which he is created." (St. Ignatius Loyola, *Spiritual Exercices*)

Many people think that God just wants us to be happy here and now. God does want us to be happy but not necessarily as we think we should be happy. God wants us to be happy in Heaven and therefore we should work at being worthy to go to Heaven.

Can we have a hint on how to put that into practice? Yes.

> "'Master which is the greatest commandment of the law? 'Jesus said to him: Thou shalt love the Lord thy God with thy whole heart, and with thy whole soul, and with thy whole mind." (Matthew 22:36-37)

Thus, the greatest commandment is that we love God back. Many Christians go around with the message that "Jesus loves you." And indeed, that is the first news of the Good News. Jesus, the second person of the Trinity, has come out of love for each one of us to suffer on the cross and gain our redemption.

However, this is only a beginning. Now we need to love God back. It is not enough to know that God loves us but we need to get going on the road of loving God back.

> "For this is the love of God, that we keep his commandments: and his commandments are not grievous." (1 John 5:3)

To love God is to keep his commandments, all of them.

One of the errors of these days is to say to oneself: "I may not be perfect but I know that God does not make junk. So, I will keep being myself imperfect." Such a person may believe that it is what his or her conscience tells them but he or she are sadly mistaken. Indeed, we need to follow our conscience that is telling us what is good and what is bad. But a conscience should be well formed and it should know about the whole context of the Good News. It is possible to have had a very distorted conscience after living a life where our conscience has been muffled down to the point that it hardly has any voice at all.

At any rate, this false attitude should be corrected in the light of the saying of Jesus:

> "Be you therefore perfect, as also your heavenly Father is perfect." (Matthew 5:48)

Our Personal Vocation

So all human beings should love God and obey His commandments. This is how to gain the spiritual merits generally. By forming our conscience and following as well as we can the prompting to do good and avoid evil we gain merits for our personal salvation.

But that may look as a vast, complicated plan. We need a few hints to be better able to put this plan in practice.

> "Progress in holiness begins with the realization that God has a providential plan for all mankind and a special vocation for me." (John Hardon, S.J. *The Catholic Cathechism*)

Yes. Even though there were billions of human beings in the past, are in the present and will be in the future, we are not numbers in the eyes of God. He made each one of us very different and for a special vocation.

In particular, God, at our conception and later in life gave us good traits that were to be developed and exercised in order to contribute to fulfill His plan of salvation for ourselves and for all human beings. Throughout our lives, God puts situations before us that will contribute to His plans for the whole of mankind and for us individually, provided we respond positively to His promptings, and that we use our very special talents for His service at any given time and in any given place.

By recognizing and responding positively to these promptings from God to do His will, we gain the merits that will assure us a place in Heaven.

However, we may agree to all of the above and still be a bit reluctant to go further on this path. We may ask ourselves: "where is this going to lead me in practice?", "I know my strong points and my preferences, should I really give them up and let God work through me blindly?" "All this is fine in the long run, but what about the immediate? I have practical issues to resolve and need to concert myself with how to resolve them?"

We understandably need to have a sense of how the responsibilities that we have every day would mesh with God's plan for each one of us.

Chapter 11 – Divine Providence

In order to help allay these concerns, we need to have a look at the nature and operations of Divine Providence.

> "[I]n God there is a providence directing all things to the good of the universe, the manifestation of divine goodness in every order, from the inanimate creation even to the angels and saints in heaven." (Fr. Garrigou-Lagrange, OP, *Providence*)

God has a plan for the good of the whole creation including, and especially, for human beings, and for each individual human. But this plan does not consist only in determining the final general objectives, as in "manifest[ing] goodness in every order", but He also takes a hands-on approach to implementing the plan, "directing all things."

In particular, God is prompting all individual human beings to be active participants in the execution of His plan for the whole world.

Why should we abandon ourselves to divine providence?

> "The answer of every Christian will be that the reason lies in the wisdom and goodness of Providence…The first of these principles is that everything which comes to pass has been foreseen by God from all eternity, and has been willed or at least permitted by Him…The second principle is that nothing can be willed or permitted by God that does not contribute to the end He purposed in creating which is the manifestation of His goodness and infinite perfections, and the glory of the God-man Jesus Christ, His only Son….
>
> "In addition to these two principles, there is a third which St. Paul states thus (Rom. 8:28): 'We know that to them that love God that all things work together unto good; to such as, according to His purpose, are called to be saints and persevere in His love.' God sees that everything contributes to their spiritual welfare, not only the grace He bestows on them, not only those natural qualities He endows them with, but sickness too, and contradictions and reverses; as in the case of Saint Augustine, even their very sins, which God only permits in order to lead them on to a truer humility and thereby to a truer love. It was thus He permitted the threefold denial of St. Peter, to make the great Apostle more humble, more mistrustful of self, and by this very means become stronger and trust more in the divine mercy." (Fr. Garrigou-Lagrange, OP, *Providence*)

So God, in His Divine Providence, is perfectly conscious of these "natural qualities" that He gives us. He does not give us these qualities randomly. He definitely means to make sure these qualities are going to be helpful in His plans but he will also send "contradictions and reverses" that will make these qualities not always effective at that moment for the sake of a higher good to be gained by each one of us individually.

To the degree that we ourselves have understood and cultivated these qualities that we have, through no merit of our own, besides the acceptance of God's prompting to use and perfect them, we should also be prepared to encounter difficulties in the mundane affairs of our lives.

God wants us to be humbler so that we understand more clearly how much we depend on him. The difficulties and reverses we will encounter will show us that we cannot be successful all the time. But the acknowledgement that the qualities He put on us are totally owed to Him can only lead us to lose all personal pride and replace it by the love of God.

Now, quickly, we should mention that there has been, in the past, a heresy called "Quietism" that taught to be basically inert before the will of God and do nothing special because God's providence will provide in all things. The error of Quietism is "that self-abandonment to God's will does not dispense us from doing everything in our power to do God's will as made known in the commandments and counsels [the spirits of poverty, chastity and obedience … that should rule how we manage our belongings, our body, and our will] in the events of life" as Fr. Garrigou-Lagrange wrote.

The good father continues: "[T]he saints would confess that fundamentally the one thing necessary is to do the will of God day to day. God never commands the impossible. Each moment has a duty which God makes really possible for every one of us and in the fulfilment of which He appeals to our love and generosity."

The understanding and appreciation of God's providence allows us to better direct our efforts as we understand that our lives have a great purpose and we each have a mission, as well as to bear with patience the difficulties that we will surely encounter in our lives. Thus, we will not be depressed by the seemingly randomness of events in our lives, nor be broken by the difficulties to be expected.

Right there is the first fruit of the purest happiness available on earth from trusting in the Lord God.

Chapter 12 - The Commandments

We must now review the Commandments of God, the Ten Commandments, that we need to follow to do God's will. We presently live in world where the Commandments have been twisted to mean something so totally different from what was initially intended by them that we can be excused if we are unable to appreciate them for their just values.

First Commandment: You shall have no gods besides me.

We shall adore only God (the author and source of all goodness and love). We should pray to God. We must sacrifice to God only as a mark of our adoration.

We may not fulfill the First Commandment if we are avoiding conscious acts of adoration that God deserves, or committing sins against the true religion of love.

The spirit of the world which is very much in opposition to the Spirit of God, keeps inciting us to basically adore people, ideas, fashions, and so forth. We can appreciate some of that if warranted, but we must reserve our adoration to God only. The false tolerance of exotic religions which is very common these days, is especially a sin against this first Commandment.

Second Commandment: You shall not use the name of God in vain.

The proper place and time to pronounce the name of the Lord is during prayer, or during serious discussions on divine matters. Vows and oaths are also times when the name of the Lord can be used. In the case of vows, it shows the vow taker to entrust the decision, the object of the vow, to God. Oaths can be used when reverently taking God as witness for a statement we make. Swears, curses, blasphemy, profanity and perjury are all sins against this commandment.

Third Commandment: Remember the Sabbath Day and keep it holy.

Just as God rested on the seventh day of creation, we should keep that day free of work and reserve it to observing ritual and personal marks of adoration for our Lord.

Fourth Commandment: Honor your father and your mother (Ex. 20:12).

The family is the basic unit of society but also a "small Church". Children should respect their parents as the founders of their families, as the heads of the family, as the providers of the families, and as entrusted by God to serve the younger and weaker members of the family and the first teachers to teach them the glories of God.

Fifth Commandment: You shall not Murder.

That Commandment is well known and most people have no problem to accept it because they understand it improperly. Most people are not murderers so the Commandment is not addressing them, they think. But any act that injures someone else is a sin under this commandment. It may injure them physically, but also mentally, morally, or their reputation. Abortion and euthanasia are sins under this Commandment. However, while the Church condemns the sinful passions which may lead to war, it affirms the permissibility of Christians to engage in a just war.

Sixth and Ninth Commandment: You shall not covet your neighbor's wife, you shall not set your heart on his house, his field, his servant – man or woman – his ox, his donkey or anything that is his (Deut. 5-21).

These are Commandments for the protection of chastity, and condemning unjust desires for someone else's goods: greed. Christians are to control sexual gratification to the proper time and place with the proper person of the other sex, and within the bond of marriage and a commitment to fidelity.

Seventh and Tenth Commandment: You shall not steal.

The Commandment against theft is usually well understood as we may all be targets of thieves every day.

Eight Commandment: You shall not bear false witness against your neighbor.

This Commandment is about witnessing in a court of law as well as in current life against someone when it is not called for; it is calumny. It is also about lying.

The first commandment of the ten commandments, those given to Moses by God on Mount Sinai, inscribed in the Tables of the Law, directs the attitude we should have before God. This is first because God's existence is the first most important reality in the whole universe but also for each one of us. Our priorities should all be in God.

But Jesus himself taught also:

> "Jesus said to him: 'You must love the Lord your God with all your heart, with all your soul, and with all your mind. This is the greatest and the first commandment. The second resembles it: You must love your neighbor as yourself. On these two commandments hold the whole Law, and the

Prophets too." (Mat. 22:37-40)

The great commandment is to love God first, and then our brothers and sisters of the human race.

Chapter 13 - The Great Crusade of Love.

From January 6, 1996 to January 25, 1996, Jesus dictated to a simple woman named Catalina from Bolivia a book that Jesus called "The Great Crusade of Love." The whole book, containing about 200 pages in the English edition, was written then in two weeks. It received the Imprimatur of the local Archbishop., meaning the certification of the Church that it does not contain doctrinal errors. Catalina is bearing the stigmata of Jesus' crucifixion on her hands, feet and head.

The messages begin thus:

"In order for each one of you to progress, My Will must be fulfilled after the soul has managed to overcome certain difficulties predisposed by Me. Think, each one of you, about yourself in the time elapsed since your conversion and do not forget that if I delayed in manifesting My Glory it was because I wanted that manifestation to be much greater. [.]

"Open your eyes, look how great the field is in which I am preparing you day by day. I promise you, you will gather from this field all the fruit that I have reserved for you if you remain faithful and steadfast."

"You, who believe in Me, leave everything to Me, because no one except Me can understand your longing, and no one except Me can appease it, since I gave it to you to call you to certain things. And if I gave you the desire, should I not know how to satisfy it?"

"Say 'enough' to your anxieties, calm yourselves, rest in My Heart, because divine harmony will be revealed if you hear only one heartbeat. [.]

"Let us sit together about the love that I want to give you, since this is the discourse that I always nourish, because you have to grow a lot in love. I tell you this because I have a particular preference for you."

"I shall help you, yes, of course I shall. But it is so that you will love Me, so that you will grow to the stature that I want to give to you all…"

Our Lord – in these terribly personal words – tells us several things:

- We have to progress up until we reach the stage of conversion before he can help us in a more particular way to progress further after we are ready to listen. The difficulties that we encounter until then are some of the difficulties presented in this book about believing in God and believing in Jesus. But he has customized these difficulties for each of us because he is interested directly in each one of us. And this statement should not lead us to believe that he does not help us from our first hours on earth to come to that first stage. He specifically says so in these messages too.

- Jesus tells us to take a look at the minute details of our lives in all their complexities, difficulties, but especially promises, both practical and earthly, as well as spiritual and religious. He is telling us that, indeed, He has a personal plan for each one of us and he will help us fulfill this plan. The good special interests and desires we possess, in a way that no other person possesses, He knows about them because he put them there. He wants to see them fulfilled. There is much to gain when we decide to follow his Will.

- Following his will is also gain total peace. He will use our abandonment to his will to work through us to bring us to the stage of development that he had reserved for us from all times.

- In all of these messages, Jesus shows how infinite is His love for each one of us. However, once we know that, this is not the end of the road nor the end of our obligations. On the contrary. Our real objective is now clear: it is to love Jesus with all our hearts, with all our minds and with all our souls. And he will teach us how to do it.

The messages also contain many wonderful things that confirm us in our faith as it shows that all the tenets support each other. They all make sense together.

For example, Jesus tells us that during his life on earth he did everything according to the will of his Father, including and especially accepting his crucifixion. This obedience to the will of the Father is a mark of the love that as the second person of the Trinity he has for his Father, similarly as the sign of the love that all the persons of the Trinity have for each other.

We all know that God is perfect and needs nothing for His happiness, but this understanding may have contributed to a serious problem: we have some difficulty in understanding that we need to love God, to grow in the love of God. We have not understood that the second person of the Trinity has taken a human nature and has the same expression of his love and the same needs for the love of others that we humans do. That should help us to better respond to the requirement to love God, for we can relate to it starting from what we understand of human love. Thus a cry like this in his messages:

> "I am thirsting to make you humble in order to give you the treasure that in vain you will seek outside of me. Do you not see how My words

> burn with so much ardor, to the point that I show that I need you, while you have need of Me? Where is he who loves Me and why do so few listen to Me?"
>
> "Tell Me, if you at least want My Love…I shall pay you by giving you more longing. I know what your heart desires, and I shall satisfy it fully by giving it the fullness of love without the shadow of concern or fear. I shall not hide from your eyes; you will see Me and will enjoy the ardor of lovers. But in the meantime, burn all your impurities; accept the works that I fulfill in your soul, and with confidence abandon yourself in Me…"

Jesus is clear on the process changing of habits for the better in order to find Him:

> "The soul is incited to love Me when I show it the beauty of the object of its search. It is necessary that I build a refuge for each one of you where you can find Me and recognize Me. Many follow false ideals and are always eager for the good that escapes them, because of the delusions with which they fill their minds and hearts. I allow Myself to be found, I manifest Myself to those who rid their souls of vices and defects, of selfishness and pride. No one will know the truth if he does not abandon that which is false."
>
> "I speak to you through created things. I attract you to Me, because I am the Light who gives sight to the blind. I am the good that satisfies."

Jesus confirms that the more he places good qualities in each one of us, the more he expects from us.

> "However, I expect more from those to whom I give more, and if I give less, I am happy with less."

Jesus is very clear on what happens to those who refuse to do His will:

> "Everyone shares these gifts, without which not only would you return to nothing, but you would never be able to receive mercy and forgiveness, like those who are condemned. They lie in the most horrible of prisons – the one of rebellion. And why? Because in life they were guided and driven by all kinds of vices. Many times I wanted to bring them to Me! They fled, making use of their own will – My supreme gift."
>
> "Remember that each one of them is an example of what man is capable of without me. Be assured that not one of them is condemned without his willingness and, just think, Divine Justice has not even cried out against them with the severity they well deserve. I am just and appease justice with My mercy."

But Jesus works full time at trying to save especially those who refuse Him. He does not give souls a second chance but millions of chances to come to Him.

> "I thirst for those who offend Me, and I want

> them to find out about their faults, because one of the principal faults that distances them from Me is ignorance. They do not know what helps or harms them. They have hardened their hearts in such a way that they have become like a rock over which the ocean waves pound. My poor loved ones, what will they do without Me? Who will take them out of their misery? I shall do it together with those who love Me."

Jesus confirms how He is acting through us as mentioned above in this book:

> "Grow and you will see that no man lives without My impulse. You cannot resist it but only by lack of love or by foolishness, thus making useless the feeling that I give." (the English version has a translation error corrected here with the help of the French version of the book).

Jesus tells us that we should follow the example of His mother who managed the joys and difficulties of life – like we do but at a much higher degree – at the highest level of perfection:

> "My Mother, as yourself, lived in this world, working, watching over the good of the people, praying … And though her soul was elevated towards God in each instant of her life, she did not for one moment leave the path of the Divine Will. She knew how to harmonize the cares and troubles of the world, in a way that they all formed a hymn of gratitude to Divinity. With her

> heart full of grief at the thought of my Future, she knew how to hide in her soul and make life enjoyable to the rest."

But things have deteriorated in the world. Many souls are being lost. Now Jesus wants the world to have the Great Crusade of Love to make things right and avoid the great chastisement.

> "My daughter, a great campaign should be drawn up, a Crusade of atonement and penance. This Crusade will be intense and constant, strong and real, and truthful and convincing. The world must prepare itself to resist the attacks of the Beast. The great tribulation is prepared and the world will cry tears of blood."
>
> "If the world prays, My reign will be closer and My Sacred Heart will pour over the hearts of men the Light and the Life of the true Love that, being infinite, springs from Me. It will show you the true way to follow with regard to your duty towards your neighbor."
>
> "All of humanity offends me; they do not want to listen to My voice, nor do they want to understand it. But My sadness is greater because even those who call themselves Mine do not want to hear it. I have asked that reparation be made, no one pays attention, they fear the 'what will others say'. While they vacillate, men continue accumulating iniquities and, as a result, greater chastisement for all humanity." [.]
>
> "The Crusade is necessary in the entire world.

Start it in this town, radiate towards other points, so that it will expand, as I wish to expand My Mercy. The word must go forth so that it moves hearts and makes a great part of humanity understand the whirlwind that has enveloped man. The road embarked upon can only take man to total destruction if he does not do penance."

The book, "The Great Crusade of Love" is available from:

In English and Spanish
www.loveandmercy.org/
Here the book is downloadable for free.

In French:
www.parvis.ch
email: book@parvis.ch.

Chapter 14 - To Be Remembered

"Left to our own powers, we could never love as God has loved us. But Catholic Christianity emphasizes that God actually invites us to participate in His divine love. Here, we come to what is arguably the most astonishing aspect of the Catholic faith. God does not just pardon us for our sins. He wants to fill us with his life. He wants to transform our hearts. He seeks to heal, perfect, and even elevate our human love, so that it participates in his own perfect divine love. This is what He has been doing throughout the centuries in the lives of countless ordinary Christians: changing our minds and hearts, so that we can begin to see as He sees, and love as He loves. Through God's grace – His divine life in us – we can begin to love in a much more profound way than we ever could on our

> own, for as Saint Paul once wrote, '[I]t is no longer I who live, but Christ who lives in me' (Gal.2:20) (Edward Sri, *Love Unveiled*).

And

> "'God loves us that we might love Him' (1 John 4-10). That is the explanation of it all: of the Creation, the Incarnation, Calvary, the Resurrection, the Eucharist. Creation, if we may express it in this way, is the infinite love that overflowed from Him. God created us out of love for Himself and out of love for His creatures, whom He made in order to fill them with His love and His mercy." Fr. Jean C.J. D'Elbee *I Believe in Love.*

Ralph Martin in his "*The Fulfilment of All Desire*" brings witness that one of the many fruits that full unity of the soul in love with God leads to fruitfulness in our works. For this he quotes St. Bernard de Clairvaux in his "*On the Song of Songs*":

> "Men and women of this kind undertake great deeds… and what they undertake they achieve in accord with the promise which runs: 'Everyplace on which the sole of your foot treads shall be yours' (Deut. 11:24). Great faith deserves great rewards; and if you step out with the trust to where the good things of the Lord are to be found, you will possess them."

Chapter 15 - Heaven

St Paul after he had been taken in rapture to the third heaven wrote:

> "Eye has not seen, ear has not heard, nor has it so much dawned on man what God has prepared for those who love him." (1 Cor. 2:9)

Father Charles Arminjon wrote a book on "*The End of the Present World and the Mysteries of the Future Life*". St. Therese of Lisieux stated: "Reading this book was one of the greatest graces of my life".

This is what Fr. Arminjon said of Heaven:

"[I]n heaven, the bliss of glory, far from rendering souls more human, elevates them and makes them more spiritual. Their awareness of happiness is not distinct from their awareness of God. The harmonies that charm their ears, the light that bathes their eyes, the aromas their enchanted nostrils inhale are naught but the power of God rendering itself perceptible to their senses. And the effect of the multifarious delight is not to induce them, by reflection, to withdraw into excessive preoccupation with themselves and the baser perfection of their nature, but, rather, to inspire them to soar upward with inexhaustible energy and lose themselves in the ever-closer embrace of God, who imbues them with His fullness through all their senses and penetrates every pore of their being. On their lips the cry of joy blends with the cry of adoration and gratitude. They do not say, like the carnal disciples, "It is good for us to be here: bonum est hic nos esse"; but they exclaim, "Holy, holy, holy is God Almighty."

About the Author

For 20 years, Jean-Francois Orsini has run the St. Antoninus Institute for Catholic Education in Business. During this time, he wrote, in addition to monthly newsletters and several annual versions of the *Pro-Life Shopping Guide, Virtue Based Management* a complete handbook of Management treated from a Thomistic perspective, explaining how to faithfully implement Catholic Social Teachings in all the very details of management. For 15 years, he has been teaching business courses at the university level, including courses of business ethics, finance and general management. He has also founded several small businesses. After high school courses including Latin and Greek as well as the heaviest quota of mathematics and science, he graduated from a top French business school, ESCP Europe, and later earned an MBA and a Ph.D. from the Wharton School. He is a third order Dominican and served two terms as prior of his Dominican lay chapter. He is a Knight of the Holy Sepulcher. Also, father of 6 daughters, he is so far grandfather of 7 grandchildren. He was born in Vietnam and grew up in Morocco and France.

Made in United States
Orlando, FL
23 March 2023